CROSSROADS

To Jim,

Poetry Now 2010

All the best with
this writing thing!

The proceeds from sales of this book will be
donated to the National Rehabilitation Hospital,
Rochestown Avenue, Dun Laoghaire.

Deansgrange Writers Group wish to thank
Dun Laoghaire Institute of Art, Design & Technology
for their ongoing support.

The production of this publication is kindly supported by:

AB Cycle Factors, Summer Street, Dublin 8
Artisan Visual Communication
A1 Computers, Johnstown Road, Cabinteely
Bakers Corner, Kill Avenue, Co. Dublin
Dawes Bikes/Trek Bikes Ireland
D.K.C Chartered Accountants
G-Print Ltd. KCR Industrial Estate, Dublin 12
Grange Audi, Deansgrange, Co. Dublin
Hill's Hire, Johnstown Road, Cabinteely
Huet Distributors, Glenamuck Road, Carrickmines
J. H. I. Cycles, Finglas, Co. Dublin
MSL Service Centre, Pottery Road, Dun Laoghaire
The Bike Rack, Johnstown Road, Cabinteely
The Grange, Deansgrange, Co. Dublin
The Patio Centre, Johnstown Road, Cabinteely

CROSSROADS

an anthology of new writing

Edited by Katie Donovan

Deansgrange Writers Group

First Edition
Published by Deansgrange Writers Group 2009
www.deansgrangewriters.com

© Copyright remains with the authors

ISBN number 978-0-9564384-0-9

All rights reserved. No part of this publication may be
reproduced, stored in a retrieval system, or transmitted,
in any form or by any means, electronic, mechanical,
photocopying, recording, or otherwise, without
the prior written permission of the publisher.

All characters in stories herein are fictitious,
and any resemblance to actual persons,
living or dead, is purely coincidental.

Designed and typeset in 11/12.5pt Garamond
by ARTISAN VISUAL COMMUNICATIONS
www.artisan.ie

Printed in Ireland by COLOUR BOOKS LIMITED, DUBLIN

Contents

AUTHOR	TITLE	PAGE
Katie Donovan	Editor's Note	7
Catherine Paradise	William and Eileen	8
Barney Power	The Lamp	17
	A Traveller's Tale	21
Chris Allen	Lute	23
	Hope	24
	My Eurydice	25
	Not Loath	26
	The Flowers are Wreaths	27
	The Art of Tenement Beds	28
Fergus Kelly	Heaven on Earth	29
	The Skinner's Horse	33
Annie O'Curry	The Lion's Den	36
Padhraig Nolan	Pickings	44
	Vessels	46
	Yard Brush	47
	Spark	48
	Kinship	49
	Replica	50
Lucille McDonald	Magic Molly and The Little People	51
Caitriona Stewart Short	Leaving Belfast 1941	60
	The House Party	62
	Frankie and Amelia	66
Tom Barrett	Bee Navigation	68
	Train Journey	71
Declan Houton	Pay Rise	75
	Her	76
	Circling	77
	The Wardrobe Monster	78
	Dark Night	80
	Adam and Eve	81
John Piggott	Crossroads	84
	The Coat	90

Katie Donovan

Editor's Note

I first got to know the members of the Deansgrange Writers Group in 2007 when I was Writer-in-Residence for Dun Laoghaire/Rathdown County Council and IADT. John Piggott, co-ordinator of the group, invited me to attend a meeting. Assuming I would be expected to comment and lead, I found myself instead drawn in to the writing activity that was part of the workshop. I ended up composing a poem of my own. The session went well for us all, and I was left with the impression of a tightly-knit, dedicated circle of writers full of loyalty to each other and to their craft.

It is with pleasure I am now introducing to the reader a selection of their writings, including poetry, fiction and non-fiction. Here is a variety of voices, drawing in politics, satire, family life, travels abroad and classical mythology. There is a ghost story about a shipwreck, a story for children about leprechauns, a memoir of the Dalai Lama, and responses to the recession in both verse and prose. Although each writer possesses his or her own distinctive style, there is, overall a confidence in tone and an ability to summon up a scene - from a crowded train station in Belfast to a lamplit farmhouse in Waterford - that makes this book consistently enjoyable and entertaining.

It was my task simply to whittle down a rather larger selection of work from each writer to the sampler you hold now in your hand. Each of these writers is prolific and talented and I wish them all the best in their future projects.

Katie Donovan

Catherine Paradise

William and Eileen

Frances became a schoolgirl in September. She'd perch on the crossbar of William's bike as he pedaled her to school. From there, William continued to his job where he worked as a motor mechanic.

Frances cried when she was left at school. She felt she'd been dumped, put out of the way. There was a meal at mid-day. Eating it was an ordeal. The meat was like rubber and Frances pushed it into a space at the side of her cheek. "Eat up my dear" urged the kindly dinner lady. In the afternoon, the class lay down on mattresses on the floor of the assembly hall and were quiet. While some of the children slept, Frances thought of 'Milly, Molly, Mandy' and other stories. She imagined herself as Alice.

The school uniform was gymslips of navy serge with white blouses. Collars and cuffs were dirty within a day. Ties threatened to strangle their owners. Liberty bodices were sometimes worn underneath. Some of the boys dipped her hair into inkwells. It was a trying time.

On Sundays the family visited Kew Gardens and, occasionally, Richmond Park. In the park there were deer grazing. They were shy and ran away when approached. Picnicking visitors were shaded by oaks and beeches. Empty fizzy drinks bottles were left for the park attendants to collect. Cucumber sandwiches were a big favourite with the park people. Long summer days encouraged tramps to live there in the open air, those strangely fresh-faced men and women with the brown carrier bags that contained all their worldly possessions. In the trees, pigeons cooed, their heavy chests threatening to topple them. Ducks, fat with unlaid eggs, waddled into the grassy shallows to nest. Frances, Eileen and William made chains from the pink tipped daisies as they ate Italian ice cream which melted and dripped down the sides of the wafer cones.

It was early May. The dew fell at night making the grass cuttings cling together in moist clumps. They'd take a tarpaulin to spread on the still-damp grass. Eileen made sausage rolls garnished with parsley. They packed china plates and cups with matching saucers. Sometimes a friendly dog would join them, her Mum and Dad always had room for strays. Frances hated it when William tickled Eileen in her ribs, the scuffle, the redness on her parents' faces.

She pretended not to see.

In the park a band played to an audience seated in deck chairs. The tramps had always secured the best seats in the house and slept soundly in them. Only when their snoring became unbearable would somebody shake them till they stopped.

The bandsmen wore navy suits and ties. Their coats were sewn with lots of shiny brass buttons. Girls with their hair in pony tails hung close to the bandstand, drawn by the uniforms like moths. A pack of dogs sniffed and barked, infected by the excitement of it all. Babies' cries added to the general din. Eileen reflected that these sights and sounds of the park were different somehow. It was a sad reality that nothing remained the same after childhood. As the evening cooled, she looked around at the couples brushing the wrinkles from their clothes as they prepared to go home.

Eileen thought what a lonely place the park must be at night. The homeless people lit illegal fires after dark. She pictured the scorched grass they would leave in the morning as she looked at William and wondered did he have an imagination. Did he think about the park at night? She thought about how you can live and share almost everything, your whole life with somebody, and never know their silent thoughts. Putting on a cardigan, Eileen discarded her inner self. She began gathering up greaseproof paper, paper bags and crusts that had become hard in the sun. The ritual signaled the end of a perfect day. How hard it was that it had to end. It occurred to her that, sooner or later, it was so with all good things.

The following morning, Eileen had an interview at eleven o'clock. It was for a job as a daily help at a large house. Working on Saturdays had been unsatisfactory. The interview went well and she was given a starting date. William wasn't pleased. He couldn't understand why she wanted to work. He brought home enough money. They were saving for a new house. But Eileen was adamant. She wanted to be independent and have some money of her own.

William went off to the pub for a pint and to grumble with his male companions about the vagaries of the fairer sex. He found he was not alone. Other wives wanted to work, for washing machines, a family holiday, a better car. Next thing, William thought, they'll be wanting to drive their own cars! What was the world coming to?

"Fancy a game of poker?" asked someone. William played and lost.

William walked home, his hands buried deep in his pockets, his shoulders shrugged. At home he banged about in the kitchen as he prepared a mug of Ovaltine for himself before bed. He slammed the bedroom door making sure he woke Eileen. She'd be tired in the morning, might make her think a little about the potential costs of these newfound ambitions of hers.

"What's wrong, William?" asked Eileen. William was hopping on one leg having banged his shin on the bedside table for the second time.

"Nothing." He harrumphed and got into bed, wrapping himself in the blankets well over to his own side.

* * * *

Next day was Saturday. Frances lay in bed looking at the sunlight dancing on the trees outside her window. Her mother had grown fatter lately and every afternoon she rested in the armchair with her legs up on a footstool. Frances was hoping William would take her to Richmond ice-rink after lunch. She was six that summer and had been learning to skate. Leaning over she reached down beside her bed for her knitting. At school they taught the girls knitting and the boys weaving on a small loom. Frances sighed. There were a great many holes in her square of plain.

Eileen came in. "Up you get. Daddy's taking you for a walk." Eileen moved around the bedroom in the timeless way of all mothers, picking up clothes and folding them in neat piles. Frances dressed in her blue spotted dress, white socks and sandals. Every year, in Spring, Frances received a new pair of rather expensive sandals.

The couple next door were elderly and childless. They would read stories to Frances, 'Billy Goat Gruff' and 'The Water Babies'. They gave her large dolls and even, one Christmas, a doll's house. Eileen said they'd spoiled her. When Frances learned she was going out with Daddy, she ran to tell them.

Frances' friends were called Mr. and Mrs. O'Rourke. He had been a jockey until a bad fall had left him with a badly damaged leg and a failed nerve. There were to be no more six o'clock rides on The Curragh for Tom O'Rourke, no more early morning excursions with high strung thoroughbreds. He became a night watchman at Twickenham film studios and married Alice, the daughter of a Dublin bank manager. In her youth, Alice O'Rourke had a governess and had learned the piano, to sew and to knit, at home. She dressed her dolls in knitted dresses for winter and cotton ones for summer.

William and Frances walked across the white bridge at Richmond and looked at all the people out shopping or for a stroll. Frances fingered a button on her cardigan. She was wearing a grey wool buttoned-through cardigan with red embroidered flowers down the front. The buttons were shaped like ducks. She was holding a child's shopping bag made of red and blue material which held crusts for the swans. The bag was a present from Tom and Alice, designed to see that Frances grew up to be a good wife and mother who would shop diligently.

William would smile at people he knew and Frances was proud of her handsome Daddy. As they strolled they'd occasionally stop to gaze in shop windows. Outside the car showrooms they looked longingly at a Rolls Royce Silver Cloud. It was pale grey. It stood alone, elegant and unobtainable.

"Why is Mummy so fat?" Frances asked suddenly.

"Your Mummy's expecting a baby," William answered.

Frances fell silent, wondering if she was going to like this new arrival.

Soon they were on the bus back to the King's Road. At home there was a delicious smell of a Sunday roast slowly cooking in the kitchen. Eileen was making gravy on the gas stove.

"Hurry up." She put down the familiar cream and green dinner plates and soon they were tucking in to the roast, pink and succulent beef with Yorkshire puddings, new potatoes and garden sprouts. Dessert was jelly and custard and afterwards William helped Eileen with the washing up. Then they went for a nap.

Frances coloured her drawing book and worked on improving her knitting. At tea-time there was bread and butter with home-made strawberry jam. Chelsea buns, golden and yeasty, sat on a doily-covered plate in the middle of the table. William leaned back dangerously far on his chair and rubbed his middle.

After tea they listened to the radio until it was time for Frances' bed at nine o'clock. Downstairs Eileen sat sewing while William sat under the standard lamp reading his newspaper. On the mantlepiece a clock of Spanish wood ticked loudly. On the hour it chimed and both of them checked the time.

"I'll have to change the car," said William.

"Well, keeping it idle and hoping it will go one day is a waste," said Eileen.

"It's a good car, maybe a little unpredictable, but a good car," William was defensive.

"Anyway," said Eileen, not lifting her eyes from her sewing "I like cycling. It's good exercise."

"Do you want cocoa?" William was getting up, as much to finish the conversation as anything else.

Eileen's voice sounded weary. "Yes please."

The cocoa was thick, dark and creamy. William loved his cocoa.

Outside the wind howled a little and it had turned distinctly colder.

"Turn off the lights and lock up, won't you?" Eileen was headed up the stairs.

Eileen slept. Frances in her divan bed dreamed of fire, of being consumed. In the bathroom a window swung to and fro, unlatched.

At two in the morning William had woken to go to the bathroom. Soon afterwards, Eileen woke, feeling the draught. The house was silent and she was filled with apprehension. Suddenly she was struggling, being pushed down into the bed. Breathing was difficult. Terror gripped her, freezing her mind, rising in her throat but she was unable to scream because there was a hand over her mouth.

In the bed beside her, her husband stirred and turned towards her, about to speak. His words were stifled by the shock of a blow to his face from a clenched fist. Shocked and confused, William peered through his own blood at the sight of a heavy-set man, half lying across his wife, a hand on her throat. Eileen was gasping.

William felt something hard pushed into his ribs. This man had a gun.

"Get up," he ordered. "Sit over there."

William did as he was told. Eileen tried to wriggle away from her tormentor but he slapped her hard. Her long blonde hair trailed in William's blood.

Frances cried out in her sleep.

"It's my little girl," said Eileen, "Oh God, you must let me go to her!"

"After." He was lifting Eileen's nightdress, inserting a denim-clad knee between her legs.

Eileen twisted and struggled. "I'm pregnant," she said.

William made to get out of the chair but the gun was instantly pointed at him.

"Sit!"

Eileen felt like a butterfly pinned to a display board, its wings unable to flutter. When it was over the man drew back and zipped up his jeans. William was still in the chair, his face buried in his hands.

"Got any money?" The intruder was almost polite. He knew they were conquered. William pointed meekly to the bedroom drawer. Somewhere in the house, next door perhaps, a door slammed. The silence, broken only by the occasional motor car, felt surreal.

Eileen lay, blood-spattered and disorientated, completely worn out. The intruder rooted in the drawer for the wallet, emptied it on the bed and took what money there was. He left them with a warning.

"Don't phone the cops or I'll have to pay you another little visit."

When he was gone William rushed to Eileen's side. She'd barely moved. He took her hand and kept rubbing it.

"There, love, it's over now. It's over." It seemed to be all he could think to say.

William dialed 999 and the police and an ambulance arrived. The casualty department filled out a report that they could find no physical traces of force, no torn or ruptured tissues.

A week later, Eileen's baby son arrived prematurely. He was perfectly formed and healthy. Eileen said that showed the insensitivity of males. She called him Henry.

Days of sunshine and picnics in the park would be replaced by endless days of darkness.

A bunch of grapes lost their bloom and developed a grey tinge in the bowl on Eileen's bedside locker. Eventually a nurse threw out the uneaten, rotting fruit.

* * * *

Two weeks after Henry's birth, Eileen was transferred to a teaching hospital in central London for psychiatric assessment and treatment. She learned things there. Like how to be a heavy smoker and how to make money selling her tranquillisers to the highest bidder.

Laura practically took over looking after William. She fussed and heated frozen dinners. She watched Frances pick at her food. "When is Mum coming home?" had become almost a mantra. Mindful of a time when he felt Laura had appeared infatuated with him, William avoided being alone with her. He brought extra work home, bits of dismantled cars covered with rust which were soon cluttering the garden.

"When are you going to get your own car going and stop riding that ridiculous bicycle?" Laura would ask.

Lily, an actress friend of Eileen's, visited. Leaning over in a cloud of 'Apple Blossom' perfume she whispered in Eileen's ear. "All men are beasts, darling."

Lily was working in a production about Anne Boleyn and she regaled Eileen with tales of her 'rapport' with the producer.

"He has an Aston Martin, you know. It's red."

"Ah, but does he have a wife?" Eileen's practicality was born of her depression.

"Well of course he does but what does that matter? He's perfect for me."

"He doesn't suck well." Eileen was looking at Henry, distracted.

"Darling, you're never breast feeding, are you? What about your figure?"

"Who cares?" replied Eileen.

After three weeks, Eileen was discharged to the care of her family doctor. She told him, truthfully, that she wasn't sleeping well.

"I wake at about two in the morning and I don't get back to sleep after that."

"Anything else?" asked the doctor, none too interested as far as Eileen could see. "Cracked nipples." She'd wanted to shock him with 'sore tits' but had thought the better of it.

The doctor prescribed a cream that did nothing at all to alleviate the razor-like darts in Eileen's breasts.

William wanted to do something kind, so he arranged a holiday for them. He hadn't been able to talk to her about his revulsion at touching her. He could barely force himself to go through the motions of love-making, managing it only with the most mechanical movements.

The back garden had been becoming increasingly like a scrap yard. When Frances cut herself on a sharp edge there, Eileen asked William to remove the rubbish. He said he would, but it didn't happen.

A week later, Eileen packed the big suitcase from the cupboard under the stairs while he was at work. She did it calmly and methodically. Eileen had set the oven timer to cook a shepherd's pie and, on the lower shelf, and egg custard was also standing, set in a dish of water. They had begun to cook, even as she sat at the kitchen table and wrote a note for him. They filled the kitchen with such a pleasant aroma.

Eileen left the note for William on the kitchen table and left the house with the suitcase, Frances and baby Henry bundled up in his carry-cot. The taxi driver recognised a woman with problems. He dropped them at Paddington and got a male passerby in a mackintosh to help her.

* * * *

"How could she just leave?" William was wailing about his loss to Laura.

"Where could she have gone?" Laura asked.

Lily said. "Good for Eileen. It's time she paddled her own canoe."

Laura doubled her nightly medication. Paul helped himself to a little extra as well. They'd all read the letter and it seemed to send ripples through their little circle. It simply read.

"I've had enough. Enough of being a non-person. Enough of being used and taken for granted around here. Goodbye William." She didn't see any need to sign it apparently.

William's mates down the pub sympathised as blokes do. "Typical – trust a woman to do something like that, eh?" and suchlike. Milk began to gather on the doorstep. William just fetched it in and it gathered in the fridge until the door wouldn't close.

Frances had slept on the ferry. Out on deck, the salt air made them gasp. A flock of seagulls wheeled and cried noisily above the foaming, churning wake at the stern. When they docked in Ireland, greyhounds, exhausted, their legs shaking, were led from the hold below.

The threesome caught a bus to Castletown Beare. Eileen had written ahead, renting a holiday home. On the bus, Henry slept soundly in his carry-cot. A man had spread himself along the back seat. He played the mouth organ and waved nicotine stained fingers at girls who pretended to be outraged. One or two of them gave him a second look. A man going home with holiday pay.

The bus stopped and they bought bags of chips and bottles of soft drinks. Eileen wiped a clearance in the condensation on the bus window to look at the cloud-topped mountains. The man with the mouth organ played 'Nancy Spain' until the bus reached its destination. The bus driver helped Eileen off the bus with her bundles and charges. It was eight thirty when they finally got to the house and she staggered inside. It overlooked the dark blue sea.

Eileen made tea for herself and Frances. She changed Henry and settled back in a chair with him resting comfortably in her arms, surprised by the bliss of all this quiet, the smacking of his lips the only sound.

It began to rain, soft, fine droplets, almost invisible. There was a fresh, distant scent from the golden gorse flowers on the hill. The sea swelled and burst into white flecks on the shore. Far off, on the Skelligs, gannets dived for unsuspecting fish that swam too close to the surface.

Barney Power

The Lamp

The old farmhouse had not changed since Willie and Janie had first moved in five years ago. Up to that, the house had been used by all the different generations of families and relations (which could have been anything up to twenty five people including babies and children.) The structure of the house hadn't changed from the previous century with the older half of it thatched and the new, more modern half, slated when a new upper storey was being added. The Rural Electrification Scheme had come and gone and the ESB team providing it just lost patience with the delay in giving the signal for them to link it up to the national mains. So they had fastened their supply cables to the gable end of the house and left. Years later it still awaited the arrival of the electricians and the builders to connect it up inside the house. Likewise the water – "Best water in Ireland, boy!" – had to be got by dipping a bucket in the nearby well. The action really needed was for someone to go down to the water levels to fit a valve and the piping necessary to bring it into the house.

Willie and Janie were married late in life and they had no family. In fact the pair of them had lived only two fields apart all their lives but because neither of their families were in favour of them marrying, the years had just passed them by. Eventually Willie's mother was persuaded to leave the old house so the way was clear for Willie to bring his new wife into his home. They got married in a quiet ceremony which, being for a mixed wedding, had been held in the sacristy of Willie's local parish church. They spent their honeymoon in Dublin and visited a few of their nephews and nieces around the city. This is when Janie met John, Willie's nephew, for the first time.

Both Willie and Janie loved horses and bred some very good hunters on the farm. They also kept greyhounds and at one stage had both a high quality champion hunter called Bright Promise, and a champion greyhound of the same name. Both were very successful, the hunter in the RDS Horse show, and the dog in the Shelbourne Park and Youghal greyhound tracks. This meant that they had to travel to Dublin quite often where John used to volunteer to help out in exercising and looking after whatever animal was being shown.

John had finished his secondary school at the time and had applied for a few jobs after sitting the Leaving Certificate exam. An invitation to stay in their house was extended by Willie and Janie, so John travelled to Waterford and turned up from the bus on a beautiful July day. He followed the sounds in the farmyard and pushed open the door to the cowshed where Willie and Janie were both hand-milking the cows. As John was quickly to learn, when the pair were milking they carried on an animated, non-stop conversation at the same time. The air in the cowhouse was heavy with the summer heat, from the cows and the corrugated iron roof, aggravated by the background drone of the flies. The cows were contentedly chewing the cud in their bails with a rhythmical sound and there was the muffled sounds of the milk being directed into the buckets by the milkers. It was an idyllic introduction to farming for John.

That night after the evening meal was finished the three of them sat in front of the open fire. Willie was a brilliant talker about the 'old days' and loved telling yarns too. Although John had difficulty understanding his accent at times, he loved listening as Willie and Janie swapped stories about local characters and happenings. When it got dark, Janie produced and lit a beautiful old-fashioned brass oil lamp which sent a warm glow around the kitchen when it got going. When he was going to his bedroom, John was given the lamp to take with him. It gave a reassuring light along the way. He found that whenever he had to use a candle instead, he had difficulty keeping it alight, especially going into his bedroom when it always blew out. It was only much later that he discovered the bedroom he was sleeping in was supposed to be haunted. Just as well he did not know about it at the time.

The days went by and gradually John settled into the routine of the farm. He wanted to learn to milk the cows. This would be a big help to both Willie and Janie in giving one or other of them a little time off. In the beginning one of them used to have to finish each cow as the other moved to the next, as the teats being milked have to be completely dried off. On the next day he would bring the milk churns to the creamery and get whatever messages he was asked to get.

Whenever there was a dance on in the local town he borrowed Willie's bicycle and cycled there. This meant he was not interfering with the running of the house or keeping anybody awake. He loved the cycle back to the house after the dance, although the darkness of the night sky took some getting used to. When he got back to the house the key was always above the door and the oil lamp was turned on very low in the kitchen. He never had any difficulty finding his way to his room.

Occasionally he would come home early from visiting relations nearby. Willie and Janie would both be up reading or doing a crossword or maybe Janie would be doing the fashion competition in the Sunday Press. This was the only competition she approved of, as there was no gambling in it which would have been against her upbringing. She was really very good at picking out the dresses in the fashion competition and had won on more than one occasion. Either of them might be reading a book or a religious pamphlet called the 'Messenger of the Sacred Heart' which came by post to the house every month. Janie used to like the stories in it.

John went everywhere that Willie and Janie went. He used to accompany them in all their travels in their cream coloured Baby Ford. Willie used to love to point out all the places where the IRA campaign was fought in the War of Independence in the Comeragh mountains. In fact Willie himself had been the victim of the 'Troubles' when a group of Black and Tan soldiers kicked in the door of the house and burst their way into his room. He had been taken as a hostage for a journey they were making to Dungarvan about twelve miles away. Willie being the eldest in the family was taken out and pushed into the back of the Crossley Tender and they held a gun to his head all the way in case they were attacked by an IRA ambush. Willie never liked to talk about the incident, but his mother often noted he never had a stammer before then, but he certainly had one afterwards. He also loved pointing out where there had been a memorable meet of the West Waterford Hunt which he used to support faithfully. His love of the chase started when he was still at school and whenever he heard the huntsman's bugle, he escaped straight out the door of that establishment and followed the hunt on foot. Every crossroads had a memory for Willie.

At the end of three happy months in Waterford John got the call to attend an interview for a job in Dublin. He returned home very reluctantly and as a result of the successful interview he commenced working in an office where he still works to this day. He got married subsequently and is a happy family man.

During the harvest season the same year Willie had organised a neighbour to cut his oats. The man brought his combine harvester to the big field and Willie was attending to the needs of the harvester, including taking the sacks of oats and stacking them all in a corner of the field. The sacks were all very heavy and shifting them was hard even for a man of Willie's wiry strength. At the end of that long day, Willie had sat down at the side of the field, feeling unwell. He never got up.

The funeral was to his local parish, the same one in which he and Janie had been married. He was buried in an old family grave which had not been used for over a hundred years and had been rediscovered only recently.

Janie was totally distraught but attempted to run the farm on her own that winter. She bought a little donkey and cart and used it to bring the feed to the herds of cattle and sheep. It was terribly hard work and it was no surprise that, when the spring came, she put the house and farm on the market and used the money to purchase a house in Dublin.

John called to her a few times. The last time he saw her she said "John, I have something I want to give you," and had then produced the lamp, the very one that had guided John to bed all those nights he had stayed with them.

"I want you to have this," she said.

His wife had remonstrated with her but Janie had been adamant.

"This is for John. I want him to remember the good times in County Waterford."

Janie herself did not last too long in Dublin. Her heart was in West Waterford and she died there in her own family house a short time later. The funeral was to her own church in Kilrossanty, and she was buried only three or four fields away from where her beloved Willie was laid to rest.

Barney Power

A Traveller's Tale

"Well, it was a great service in the church, thank God. There must have been hundreds turned up. Tomorrow will be even bigger with the burial."

We all went inside the house and started emptying our pockets of mass cards and other messages we had received, and the letters which went with them. Some of the family busied themselves with tidying the house and doing the chores in preparation for the big crowds expected the following day.

"We'd better get some one to mind the house tomorrow when we're all out at the burial" someone suggested "It's a favourite time for burglars. They know they have about three or four hours and they can help themselves."

It certainly seemed a good idea as the house was about two miles from the town and there were no other houses close by.

"It's OK," said Frances, one of the daughters, "I'll organize someone."

The rest of the afternoon was taken up with people making phone calls to friends who might not have seen the death notice in the local or in the national newspapers and also in the preparation and stocking up of drink and food for any callers to the house. There seemed to be an unending supply of sandwiches being prepared, thick slices of freshly cooked ham jammed between great hefts of new-baked bread. Everyone was preoccupied with their own sad thoughts as they went about their chores.

"I've got someone to mind the house," announced Frances triumphantly as she came in. "Limerick Stevens."

"But you can't have him!" we all said with one voice. In the 1930s, a very liberal minded town council had set aside an area for the housing of what are now called Travellers, and built about twenty houses for them. The Travellers moved in, but struggled to retain their traditional ways. In time the terrace of houses had to cater for the Travellers' horses, pots and pans, sinks, baths and much more bric-a-brac. It was said that the attics in the terrace were accessible from one end of the twenty houses to the other and if the police were looking for stolen goods, they always started first on that terrace. In some cases the ceilings of the houses, unable to stand the weight of all the pilfered lead pipes and copper cylinders, had simply collapsed. Many of the Travellers were related to each other, and more intermarried. The social workers had great difficulty sorting it all out. Limerick Stevens was a senior member of this community and he himself had a chequered past. He had spent some time in England, mostly in the building trade, and was supposed to have 'done time' there for beating somebody up. He was also supposed to have done some boxing. This led to his being treated with no little respect among his relations and neighbours.

"Why not?" asked Frances. Nobody managed to come with a solid reason for rejecting him and so at about seven o'clock in the morning of the burial, Limerick turned up outside the house and then went into the yard. Although we invited him inside he refused, insisting instead on taking up a position among the trees outside the yard gate. I went out to talk to him and to find out if there was anything he needed. It was impossible not to notice his stocky build and the firm body of a boxer or a wrestler.

"Not a thing," he said, then added, "You know I really loved that old lady - she was always so good to me and to all my family. Now let ye all go on about your funeral and I will stay here for as long as I'm needed."

We all went to the funeral, which took a long time, the service being generously interspersed with fulsome eulogies to the deceased, followed by the burial in the graveyard a few miles outside the town. The family had organised a lunch for the funeral party at the local hotel. Most adjourned there for the meal and for drinks afterwards, where there was more meeting with relations and friends. It must have been about six o'clock when the main party returned to the house for rest, refreshments and more reminiscences. I went outside to meet Limerick but he seemed to have disappeared. Then I heard a slight rustle and he materialised as if by magic, from a thicket right beside me. He looked frozen. I noticed he was not wearing any kind of warm clothing. I asked him had he eaten and he assured me that he had plenty to eat. I asked him to come into the house anyway, for a bite to eat and for a warm-up drink, but he refused, saying, "I knows my place."

Then, Limerick Stevens went back to his vantage spot outside the gate and kept his vigil until the last guest had finally gone.

Chris Allen

Lute

Six grey hairs of my mother
Strung across the polished bone
of my father's hollow girdle.

It is a deep song out of the pelvic throat
Scripted in the marrow.

Chris Allen

Hope

Reign of ash and shadow in the east
The deep night opens over evening
Folds of dark fold further in to dark.

In that book is written for this night
How life is to begin the stoking now
To sing an utter and a merciless note.

Deep and over-amplified like a fact
The melody of squalor howling love
Is set out in the throat of a risen lark.

Chris Allen

My Eurydice

(for Dave)

I see you smile -
Your smile is like my own
Seated in the eye
Not simple to know

I see you smile -
The swallowed sadness
Not easy to hold
In the palm of my hand

I see you smile -
Tear-stained brother
Home in a room
In the mirror.

Chris Allen

Not Loath

I was busy at Thebes – Tiresias came too late.

I cannot decide if the dead envy him his breath
or he them, their situations - given the choice

to see or not to see, is - after all
the trouble of existence - the vital question

he asks not
if I have made the blessings.

I want to go to the cellars and to the attic
to sift through all the old stuff of the past.

Scour memory in search of reason.

Chris Allen
The Flowers are Wreaths

To say things that cannot otherwise be said -
A seed gestates where soon the flowers grow

And eloquence is dumb with understanding
Her perfect tongue wakes in a crocus mouth.

Chris Allen
The Art of Tenement Beds

(for Lizzie)

Hardly a stone at all like Kevin's bed -
Or Fionan's rock on Skellig
with the quilted winds.

Your Calvary to carry into myth
Worn on your flesh - my flesh
imagined in it

Blessed by the looping stitches -
Four rough sacks held fast
in the name of the Father

And of the Son -
And your six lovely daughters
so wondrously signed for love.

Fergus Kelly

Heaven on Earth

March, 30th 2008 - Today's press headlines:

"Thousands of Armed Chinese Troops Pour into Tibet";

"Turmoil in Tibet - BBC reporter says more than 400 vehicles were seen heading to Tibet through mountain passes in Western China";

"China accuses Dalai Lama, who fled Tibet in 1960, of inciting current protests in Tibet. The Exiled Spiritual Leader says he favors a peaceful resolution to the issue of greater autonomy for the remote Himalayan enclave";

"Communist party chief of Tibet says Dalai Lama is a wolf in monk's robes, a devil with a human face, with the heart of a beast."

(Reuters)

July 16th, 1935

The 14th Dalai Lama was born of a peasant family in 1935, in North Eastern Tibet. When the previous ruler passed away that year, the Tibetan government set about finding a successor. In 1937 after an extensive search, a two year- old- child in a small far- flung village in the province of Amdo, exhibited all the responses and signs required to convince the search party of high Lamas and dignitaries that the reincarnated Dalai Lama had been found.

September 9th, 1951

The Chinese invaded Lhasa, in advance of which the young Dalai Lama and his entourage were forced to flee the Tibetan capital, to a safe haven in Dharmsala, Himachal Pradesh, Northern India.

As anticipated by the Tibetan Government, the Chinese had planned to capture him en route, so a number of decoy travelling groups, spread throughout the Himalayas, created sufficient confusion to enable the Dalai Lama reach his new hideaway in India safely. His escape, I recall, caught the attention of the world, with reports being carried daily in our local press at the time. It was seen then as a modern day version of the Biblical Flight into Egypt.

July 16th, 1961

"If Ever There Was Heaven On Earth, It Is Here, It Is Here." A sign in Gurmukhi, the East Punjab script, was drawn to my attention in the vast Himalayan forest as I approached the Tibetan hideaway of His Holiness, the Dalai Lama, Ruler of Tibet.

Prit Singh Mann, a close friend and myself, accompanied by bearers, had set out at dawn by jeep from Dharmsala, in the foothills of the Himalayas, to visit the Dalai Lama. The last, most difficult and seemingly endless part of our journey through the vast deodar cedar and pine tree forests in the snow capped mountains had to be accomplished in the final stage by trekking with guides.

I had been staying with Prit and his family at their tea plantation in Dharmsala for a 'few days break' away from the hot Punjab plains. During my stay, one evening it was suggested that I might like to visit the Dalai Lama, a mere thirty or more miles into the distant mountains.

Throughout our trek to where the Dalai Lama resided, we were constantly checked and under scrutiny in the forest by Tibetan guards, whose duty it was to protect his Holiness from his enemies and unwanted intruders.

At the security entrance to where he resided, we were escorted to a small room where initially we met His Holiness's sister. After an exchange of courtesies, explanations for our visit et cetera, she draped the traditional white scarf around my neck and escorted me to the rear of the main building to an open patio-like area. Respectfully I bowed in greeting to his Holiness and placed the scarf over his shoulders. At this point he invited me to join him in prayer using the Buddhist prayer wheels.

We then sat and talked for a while during which he told me that he was celebrating his 28th birthday on that day. I was overawed and very honoured and lucky to witness this very special occasion. I was further elated to find that his Holiness did not return to me the white scarf which I had placed around his neck, conscious that this was a sign that he was comfortable in my presence as a friend and a person without threat.

Autumn 1993

I was seated aboard a Singapore Airlines aircraft awaiting departure from Delhi to Singapore. To my surprise the Dalai Lama and his entourage of lamas, and officials embarked and took up a number of reserved seats close by to where I sat. I had been aware earlier from activity in my hotel in Delhi that he had addressed a meeting in Delhi that evening prior to leaving on an official visit to Singapore. My immediate instinct was to scribble a brief note for his attention recalling my first meeting with him and wishing him well on his forthcoming visit to Singapore. This I passed to one of his aides only to be advised that I would be able to meet His Holiness prior to our arrival in Singapore next morning after he had some rest. Needless to say I never slept a wink on the flight. My wish was granted some hours later when I saw the Dalai Lama look towards my seat number and with a big smile he beckoned me to come and sit beside him. What a proud moment for me, one I will not forget. Among the many issues we discussed, I recall him telling me that we in Ireland were very fortunate in having our independence, as his country had been stolen from him. On the lighter side he told me that his favourite TV programme was *Mr. Bean* - obviously for a student with limited English at that time this had particular appeal!

September 19th, 1995

Turn the globe in a south westerly direction to the Caribbean Islands and to Port of Spain, Trinidad. As I left the Hilton Hotel to enter a taxi taking me to a business meeting, I noticed a flurry of activity at the main hotel entrance. The Dalai Lama emerged, surrounded by his lamas and security personnel. I found myself standing a matter of just yards from him when he recognised me and walked towards me with outstretched hands and a beaming smile and just simply said "How you? How you?" We chatted for a few moments before saying goodbye.

I could boast and say I felt like a long lost friend, and then why not, after all His Holiness's commitment is to make as many friends worldwide, which he has done so well to date. And of course the number of his friends if nothing else must exceed those of his enemies.

And so I ask, after more than 57 years, is there special significance in another of today's headlines?

"US President urged to request his Chinese Counterpart to have talks with Dalai Lama."

Are Tibetans still to be abused, and oppressed? Would the world stand by and let any other nation or people be treated in this manner today - I doubt it.

For Tibet it seems, nothing has changed.

Fergus Kelly

The Skinner's Horse

"I say old boy, would you like to join Major Pudumjee and our chaps for drinks at the Mess this evening?" This was an invitation not to be refused.

India had followed Ireland's example and declared Republic status in 1947. The officers of the great Indian Skinner's Horse Regiment, had served under British officers and not surprisingly therefore acquired all the 'proper' mannerisms and expressions, even growing handlebar moustaches in some instances!

Brigadier Michael Skinner commanded this elite cavalry regiment, founded by his great-great-grandfather, James Skinner, son of a Scottish father and high caste Rajput mother whom he had captured in battle. In the then early 19th Century because of his mixed blood, the young Skinner could not be commissioned in the British Army but after proving his military skills fighting with the Mahrattas, he was asked to form his own cavalry corps, which subsequently achieved major distinction on the battlefield. The Skinner's Horse had its cavalry replaced by armoured tanks early in the 20th century and following many border battles emerged as India's leading tank regiment. It had for its strength a large number of British Churchill tanks, which the officers were proud to tell everybody.

Admission as an accepted 'member' to the trophy adorned air-conditioned Officers Mess, as an outsider was a privilege bestowed on only a few. The bar, with real saddles instead of stools, reflected its great tradition as a cavalry regiment. Membership however required doing the 'test' which had been undoubtedly contrived by the officers as a Mess ruling. Yes, one had to pass the test!

On this particular July day it had been very hot and humid, with the temperature reaching forty five degrees centigrade and humidity in the high eighties. Prickly heat, an irritating skin rash, caused by excessive perspiration, had left me in a sorry state in the run up to the rainy season. This added to my overall discomfort, exacerbated by a need to get into a cool environment with a cold beer or more inside me! The Mess was the only watering hole in our region and was highly preferable, to pouring my own drinks, sitting alone, harassed by mosquitoes, beneath a noisy and ineffective fan on my verandah.

The Mess, located a mile or less from where I lived, in Nabha, Punjab was the ideal place to be heading for. My residence, Bir Niwas, a former hunting lodge of the local Maharajah, had rooms with high ceilings and tiled floors, all aimed at providing a cooler environment for its occupants. The bedroom ceiling fan, was as always a lifesaver, but only when we weren't suffering the all too frequent power cuts!

I was one of a small number of so called 'UK chaps' befriended by the officers of the regiment. Their generous invitations to regimental functions, were reciprocated by us with invitations to our frequent corporate garden receptions, et cetera.

This evening as I approached the bar, appropriately dressed of course, I received as always, a warm welcome from the Major. "What would you like to drink dear boy"? followed by a sharp order in Punjabi to the barman *"Doh burra pegs mantha Mister Das, jaldi caro!"* "Two large whiskeys Mister Das and don't delay!"

I had been a frequently invited visitor since my arrival in India some months earlier, but what I did not know was that tonight was to be the occasion of my initiation to membership when I would be subjected to the infamous 'test' in the presence of all the Officers.

The Major now ordered two *burra* - large beers - and whiskeys 'for the Sahib'. The beers I was first 'encouraged' to down with undue haste. They then swivelled my saddle clockwise seven times, followed by seven turns anti-clockwise. The whiskeys were then to be consumed in similar fashion when I was again subjected to the rotating saddle treatment.

I thought this was great fun only to hear the CO order *"Sahib mantha ek aur burra wallah, Mister Das!"* "The Sahib will have another large one, Mister Das!"

At this point I couldn't care, I felt great. Following a repeat of the drink and rotation drill, I had to dismount, keep my eyes fixed forward and walk backwards to the far corner of the room, without looking to either side. My end destination was to be a kitchen-type chair in the corner on which I was to sit securely, without the assistance of my hands or a look or glance backwards!

When I began to see the walls of the Mess shift from side to side, I thought "God, will I ever make it?" But it must have been the Irish in me that kept me on my feet. Shakily I got there and with, great aplomb, sat squarely on my by now sweaty butt to a great cheer and shouts of *"Shabash sahib-bot aitcha,"* "Well done Sahib, great stuff."

"Mister Das, aur peg Burra Sahib mantha" – "Mister Das, another peg for the great Sahib."

I was in, I had passed the test and now it was my turn to honour the regimental tradition with the call *"Burrah pegs for the officer Sahibs Mister Das, jaldi caro!"* "Large ones for all the officers, Mister Das and don't delay!"

Late that evening I was transported home, on the instructions of the CO, in a manner that even Churchill himself might approve, astride a low slung, twenty- five- foot bogey tank transporter, hanging on for dear life, to a send off of *"Shabash Sahib."* "Well done Sahib."

The joy of it all was, of course, I felt no pain.

Annie O'Curry

The Lion's Den

Lying in bed, I could hear the sound of letters dropping through the letterbox. I wondered if I would summon up the courage to open today's post. No doubt there would be the usual pile of bills and final reminders. Possibly there might be even a few cheques returned due to insufficient funds in my account. That afternoon I picked them up and stuffed them into the hall-table drawer. You see this was a little game I played. I had refused to open the post ever since I had become a victim of the recession.

Redundancy brought more changes than I could have imagined. A year ago I had a large salary, backed up by bonuses and a top-of-the-range Audi. Then one Friday evening, about four o'clock, Karl McGoldrick, the MD, sent an email to say he would like a meeting with me in his office. "What the hell does he want?" I asked myself. No doubt it was yet again something to do with targets. It could even involve my expenses, which I admit were usually on the high side. I was concerned, as it would not have been the first time the company had brought this little matter to my attention.

Thirty minutes later, I pressed the poster red button in the lift for the fourth floor. I had prepared my defence. Whatever he had on his mind, I knew I could bluff my way through it. After all I was in Sales and I knew I could talk my way through anything.

As soon as I walked into his office the first person I saw was Suzanne O'Reilly, head of Human Resources, sitting in an officious manner by his side. At once alarm bells started to ring. I had only seconds to get my bearings and work out what the hell was going on. There was a cold silence in the room until Karl looked over his Buddy Holly-style glasses and said, in his plummy voice:

"Ruth, thank you for coming up to my office at short notice. I have asked Suzanne to sit in on the meeting because the news is not good. To get to the point. The recession has taken its toll on the company and our Sales figures reflect it. Therefore it is with much regret that I have to formally deliver you with notice of redundancy as of today."

"Who me? You can't be serious!" "Ruth, we are indeed, very serious about this matter. This decision has not been taken lightly."

"I just don't believe it!"

"Well I'm afraid you have no choice Ruth. You must accept what I am saying."

"How can you do this to me - me of all people?"

Maybe it was the humidity in the room or maybe I was in shock but I could not remember one word he said after that. I began to wonder if I was in a dream as I gazed out the window at the rooftops which shimmered in the distance. I had so many questions that needed answers. Why me? After all I had been with the company for more years than most. McGoldrick explained how my time with the company would be reflected in my redundancy package which due to the difficult trading circumstances of the current economic climate, would only be statutory redundancy. I tried to do a quick calculation of how much I was due having worked for years with the company. Despite the fact that I had always been good with figures, I could not work out my package. After a while I heard him say:

"You are aware that the Human Resource Department will organise everything? If you have any further questions please do not hesitate to contact Suzanne."

As I turned to walk out of the office the plummy voice addressed me again:

"I must also remind you that there is the small matter of the keys of your company car and also your mobile. All company property should be returned before you leave the building."

'My car,' I thought. How dare he. How did he expect me to get home? I felt like asking him if he wanted to take my house as well. I was all too aware that there was a huge mortgage outstanding on it. Thanks to having bought it during the Celtic Tiger years I was now in negative equity. I also had several maxed out credit cards which had lately begun to cause me concern.

I took the lift straight to the ground floor where I knew I could smoke outside the back door. I tried to steady my shaking hands as I struggled to light the cigarette. I thought of my old school friend Sasha. Together we had danced and laughed our way in and out of our teenage years. She started in Sales two years before I joined the company. She was made redundant six months ago.

As I inhaled I tried to stay calm. Oh my God what was I going to do? I needed money to live on, did McGoldrick even stop to think of that? Unfortunately I was one of those people who, no matter how much I was earning, could not live within my means. I figured that was what others did. I was always a fun time girl. I was all too aware I was pushing twenty nine. I had to knock the best out of life while there was still time.

The weeks faded into months and I got used to the fact that my numerous job applications rarely materialised into interviews. There were days I did not want to get out of bed. In fact there were days I did not get out of bed. My local job centre said there was nothing going in Sales and advised me to consider retraining.

I began to think of the opportunities that had passed me by over the years. I had a place in university at eighteen. I was more interested in making money and had accepted a Sales job with a mobile phone company. I did very well there before moving on to another mobile phone company. After eighteen months I was headhunted by an international corporate. I had become ruthless and would do whatever it took to nail targets. I was promoted. Then I took a year out and went travelling around Australia.

When I returned to Ireland I walked straight back into a job with an American computer company as head of their Sales team. The company rewarded me for both setting and achieving targets. Above all I loved beating the men at their game. Of course there was pressure but a few drinks after work would help me deal with that too and at the end of each quarter my name was always heading up the awards list. I was earning a lot of money and I had the house and lifestyle to prove it.

It was in April last year it all began to change, just at the end of the first quarter after our figures had been reviewed. Initially I told myself I just had a bad month, but one month followed another and it was becoming impossible to hit targets. McGoldrick would not listen. I knew that my colleagues were struggling as much as I was. We blamed the economy but again nobody would listen. Management pressurised us relentlessly, insisting we reach impossible targets. Reports were requested about reports, and there were meetings about meetings. Looking back on it, I was not dealing as well as I thought with the pressure. I knew I was smoking too much. I was working six days a week and not getting home until late. There was no down time. If I was not suffering from my ulcer it was migraine. I was on a cocktail of tablets, and all self-prescribed.

I was to be found most nights drinking in the pub. I was aware that I was spending most of my money on alcohol and not enough on food. At least a few drinks guaranteed the perfect form of escape.

There was always a few familiar faces down in the pub. One Thursday evening however there was one that was not so familiar. He sat at a distance on the other side of the bar. I was aware I had a way of attracting men. I was always game. I'd say he was close to thirty five. He was on his own too. After a while he began to smile at me or was it just my imagination? Then he spoke to Tony the barman, and sent me over a gin and tonic. This took me by surprise and in the end I don't know who was smiling at whom but after a while he came over and we got into conversation.

"Thank you for the drink!" I said.

"It's always a pleasure to buy such a pretty girl a drink," he smiled.

I noticed little things like how his teeth were so white. He had nicely manicured nails and he wore very expensive shoes. I like a man that looks after himself. He wore several gold rings and of course the standard Rolex.

"Mind if I join you?"

"That would be my pleasure," I replied noticing the last word was just a teeny, bit slurred or was it just my imagination. He introduced himself as Zoltan from Budapest. In turn I introduced myself as Ruth from Dublin, which he pronounced 'Root'. Then we both laughed. He could talk but unlike most men he was a good listener too.

We chatted over a few more drinks and after a while he suggested we go out for a meal. I had not eaten all day. I was in the humour to be wined and dined, but I also reckoned he was the type of guy who expected a return for his investment.

Zoltan's car - the latest series BMW - was parked in front of the pub. It was sleek and silver with a 2009 plate. 'Who can afford a new car in the middle of a recession?' I wondered, despite my thickening alcohol-induced haze. As he started the engine, he reached for the gear stick but instead I felt his warm hand on my leg. Then he slowly kissed my cheek and said: "You know you are very lovely, Root." He put the car in gear, and, with a roar of the engine, we took off into the night.

The car pulled up outside a little Italian restaurant. A little brass bell tinkled as we walked through the door. I told him it reminded me of a restaurant I had once been to in Venice, my favourite holiday destination. It was the most romantic city in the world.

"Venice is the city of lovers. Some day I will take you there," he promised. I laughed and then we laughed together long and loud.

"Buona Sera," the head waiter greeted Zoltan. He led us to a quiet corner and produced the wine list, followed by the menu. The waiters appeared to recognise Zoltan, which was possibly why we were served drinks on the house at the end of the night.

"Your place or mine?" Zoltan flashed one of his seductive smiles as we got back to the car.

Panic set in momentarily when I thought of the pigsty that was my home. I agreed to go back to his apartment, which, much to my surprise, was not empty when he turned the key in the door. In fact there were several attractive Asian women drifting from room to room with vaguely knowing smiles. This plush apartment, decorated in red and gold felt more like a lion's den than it did a bachelor pad. I wished I'd not had quite so many glasses of wine, but then I remembered I was out to enjoy myself. I followed Zoltan down a dimly-lit corridor. Reaching for my hand, he led me through a door with a sign that read, 'Strictly Private'.

Once inside his room he fixed me another drink. After that everything seemed to slowly dissolve into a bit of a haze.

Hours later I woke up in his bed. I was shocked. I was alone. 'I have to get out of here,' I thought. Bloody hell! Where are my clothes. How did I ever get myself into this mess. Men, I found all men were the same after you slept with them, they somehow disappeared.

"Zoltan!" I called, first in a low voice and then more desperately.

"ZOLTAN . . . . !"

The door opened. The man looked different in the cold light of day. His pockmarked, olive skin now too obvious. He looked tough. He looked a lot older too and his suit looked cheap and shiny.

"Where are my clothes?" I pleaded shivering with the cold.

"Here are your clothes!" he shouted throwing the wardrobe door open revealing rails of erotic black and red lingerie, the sort of gear only prostitutes wear. "These are your working clothes. You passed the interview with flying colours, Root-my-darling! Work for me now and forget about looking for a job. No more worries, I'm going to look after you from now on."

"You take a lot for granted, Zoltan what-ever-your-name-is! What the hell makes you think I'd ever work for you?"

He was obviously not used to being rejected.

"If you're not interested, get your ass out of here fast!" he shouted.

"Go to hell!" I shouted back. "I will never work for you or any man again!"

He slammed the bedroom door. I slammed the bathroom door. I pulled on my jeans and stuffed my feet into my boots. To calm my rapid heartbeat I took several, long, deep breaths before staggering down the shady corridor to the hall door. This time there was no sign of Zoltan. My last hurdle was to walk past a dangerous looking foreign woman who looked as if she had not seen daylight in years. She was determined to see me off the premises.

Standing at a crossroads in the brilliant, early morning sunshine, lanes of traffic sped past me. Gradually I worked out I was somewhere on the northside of the city. Everything tumbled through my head. I panicked. Could I be pregnant? My stomach heaved again as I thought, "Oh my God, 'STD'?"

Contraception was fine but only if you remembered to take it. Whatever he had slipped into my drink had also left me with a blinding headache. The bastard. I checked my wallet. I had barely enough cash to call a taxi and get the hell out of this part of the city.

I continued to drink over the following weeks. I also ignored the post. The phone rang on and off but I did not answer it as I knew it could be the bank manager. He had also started leaving messages on my mobile. I simply deleted each one.

When eventually I sobered up I realised I could no longer go on living a lie. I knew I had to get a job, any job and fast. I was now desperate for money. There were no jobs going. I figured maybe I should start up my own business but what sort of business?

If things went on like this I was conscious I could lose my home. Eventually I snapped out of my daydream when a 'ping' heralded a text from Sasha on my mobile. She wanted to meet. She had so much to tell me.

The following night I went over to her place for supper.

"Well Sasha, tell me what you are you up to now?"

"Ruthie, you won't believe it. I am actually self employed. Believe me I will never work for anyone else again," she said tucking her elegant legs under her on the luxury, leather couch.

"Come on Sasha, tell me what are you doing? Don't you dare keep me in suspense!"

I stopped laughing when, flicking back a sheaf of her ash blond hair, she revealed:

"I'm working as an escort girl. And I only work with top class clients. They are the ones with the money you know, doctors, lawyers and of course some very, very well-known politicians."

"No!" I shouted in disbelief. "Tell me who!"

"No names, but you better believe it."

"Tell me please! I promise not to tell a soul!"

Sasha explained how she had a friend in the business. This friend advised her how to set herself up. She explained it was all about renting an apartment and screening clients on your mobile. The golden rule in this business is that you do not work for anyone else. That's when it gets complicated, sometimes even nasty.

"Would you consider it Ruthie? There's serious money to be made. And your hours are your own."

"Well, now you have me thinking Sasha. God knows I could do with the cash. Could I go in with you, you know, could we go into business together? I really feel you're one of the few people I could trust. What's it really like when you're starting out?"

"All you need is to take a few drinks early in the evening, that dulls the senses, and gets you through it. Just keep thinking of the money you are earning. Above all that's what motivates me. My mortgage is paid every month. I have cleared all my debts. I now have plenty of cash in the bank. In fact I have an amazing lifestyle."

She'd got me thinking. For weeks I could not get the escort business out of my head. If it worked for Sasha then it could work for me. I could see Sasha was enjoying being her own boss. I was aware I had decisions to make. I just needed a little more time.

I would talk it over with Sasha again. I know we could work well together. I liked the fact too that it was a cash business. Yet I was no fool, I was aware it could be dangerous, very dangerous.

Yes, I realised I would be living life on the edge, but then I felt I had lived like that ever since my father walked out on us all those years ago. As my mother used to say: "all men are bastards!" Why else did she have to keep two jobs going for years just to pay the bills? This would be one way of getting my own back on the world. I would rip those bastards off. This could be the very opportunity I had been waiting for. It would buy me a sort of freedom in more ways than one.

I reached down by the side of the couch for my handbag where I found my mobile phone. I scrolled through my list of contacts, searching for Sasha's number. At last I knew what I must do.

Padhraig Nolan

Pickings

Airbus sirens down to land,
Big Ben gongs a gilded mime to life,
below book barrows under Waterloo
a jackdaw worries slack, black tyre

ferry-shed in foreshore mud.
He's after something,
                        know the gulls
gliding in to gather by his side –
ganging up, sea-raptor-eyed.

Then black and white united
snap to flight.
               Here comes a man,
tidewalking, rake in hand,
heavy-wellied, knee-protected

squelching cyborg from the waist down;
backpack strapped above,
sharp eyes comb
the river's mucky hem.

CROSSROADS

Maybe every twenty strides
he crouches,
draw-rake hooked, scratching
through the ecotone - for what?

Does he seek out history or life?
Coin or clinker? Cockleshell or crab?
Paydirt or fish parasite?
Which ology is brought to bear

on gravel sliced apart for introspection?
Fiddled with and riddled, until
lapping tide insists that he unsquat,
to once again resume that shuffle stride

and I return to drop a coin
for Milligan's memoir;
pocketing this book of youth,
my South Bank prize.

Padhraig Nolan
Vessels

The bevelled hoops of the cooper
skirted staves of Russian Oak,
charred to fit and hug one form
to another upon tresses being lifted.

The crumbing knife made good the fit
to hold fresh water by the gallon
over sea to Tuskar, Fastnet and all

to the gratitude of the Lighthouse Commission,
the men of the Ballast Board
and the owners of one small cow in North Mayo
whose dash churn was also on the way.

Padhraig Nolan

Yard Brush

Old friend, I know you longer than my wife.
I brought you from my parent's home – a gift,
for you were on the way out – your acolyte
had deemed you ill-equipped. Yet here you are

your handle slick and sheened by years
of palms that regularly furled to working fists –
though woodworm traffic in your cambered
head suggests a cheese particularly Swiss.

Your nylon bristles, once bright cherry red
and eager as a pup's tumescent tip,
now clogged and grey like ancient natty dreads,
are still upstanding – equal to the chore.

At least to any I might now inflict,
for that you labour still speaks volumes too.
My yardwork (yes, the scarcity of it)
has kept our union true.

Padhraig Nolan
Spark

    rain is easy
    brushes everyone
    regardless

    thunder alluring
    comes on strong
    moves on

    lightning
    jealous lover
    mates for life

Padhraig Nolan

Kinship

I reach the bus stop just in time
and as it heaves to kerb,
out of the crease of my right eye I spy
a straggler, fellow traveller,
whose sprinting prowess sadly equals mine
(I know, I've had it tested over time).

The knot of queueing comrades
loosens slightly – not enough to merit comment.
Not a look is shared, no vowel formed
yet we conspire to tardiness in doublechecking change,
a creased brow here, a pocket rummage there;
the muting of an iPod volume, whiskerlick of hair.

At last, two steps behind the pace,
our litter's runt has boarded
to clutch the pole and tender shakily the fare
offer panting 'thank you' to the driver –
as is fair – for he's our co-conspirator,
masked by his role-requisite stare.

Padhraig Nolan
Replica

Injecting liquid plastic
the resin flows into
blood vessels, sets
to perfectly detail

all paths of circulation
each fine capillary
cast clear as all those
bare branch tips

contrasted crisply on
November's velvet dusk.
The cost? Unlike
the loss of leaves

we trust to see
regenerate in Spring,
the tissues of the heart
must be dissolved.

Lucille McDonald

Magic Molly and The Little People

As the children entered the kitchen one wet January afternoon, their grandmother was singing:

"Trasna na dtonnta, dul shiar, dul shiar"

"What are you singing, Nan?" asked seven year old Roisín.

"Over the waves and far away my child."

"Please Nan, could you tell us one of those far away stories today?" piped Oisín, his eyes shining bright as he hugged her.

"Oh! Oisín, you're only three and too little to know about far away stories," sighed Roisín.

Nan smiled, "If there's no fussing or fighting, we'll see what happens."

The children loved Nan's stories, and knew they would have a surprise.

After lunch, they snuggled up on the couch with Sukie, their golden retriever, in the middle. There was not a squeak to be heard when Nan joined them.

"In a time gone by," she began, "there was a boy named Oisín and his sister Roisín who had a Nanny called Molly. She wore colourful clothes and had a big bag filled with potions and all sorts of goodies and a flask hung from her hip. The children loved her. Molly took them on wonderful adventures right from their own couch.

"Now before we leave children," Molly began, "I want you to listen to what I have to say very carefully."

They both stared at her, with their full attention.

"On our travels you are not to eat or drink anything anyone offers you, unless I sprinkle it with my potions, is that clear?" asked Molly.

Roisín scrunched her face, "Why, Molly?"

Oisín pouted and looked at Roisín in agreement, "Yeah, Molly, how come?"

Bending over and looking straight into their eyes, she said "For if you do, you will not return."

In unison they replied, "We won't Molly, we promise."

Then she would tell them to close their eyes and remind them to keep them closed real tight, so they could imagine where they were going. She would leave their dog behind to mind the house. Then with a touch on her beautiful brooch and her magic words "*Trasna na dtonnta*," she whished them across the ocean with her special powers that allowed her not only to change their shape and size but to travel to other places and different times....

When they opened their eyes it was night-time and the moon was shining brightly. The stars lit the whole sky so it was hardly dark at all. They were in Tír Na n'Óg, *fa-dó, fa-dó, fa-dó*.

"Sshhh!" whispered Molly "What's that I hear?"

The children listened. They could scarcely make out the sound at first. It came from low down in the grass, somewhere nearby. They would hardly have called it a voice, except for the presence of words, and a jaunty little rhythm.

Molly urged them to listen harder. Having to keep quiet made listening all the more exciting.

"*Dilín ó deamhas, ó deamhas; dilín ó deamhas ó dí,*" sang a tiny voice.

Tiptoeing very carefully around the base of a big oak tree, the children could hardly believe their eyes.

On top of a mound that lay between the roots of a very old tree sat a group of tiny men. They were no bigger than Oisín's first teddy bear that he used to squeeze into his coat pocket. Roisín thought how well they would fit in her doll's house. They wore funny red, green and black hats. They all had green waistcoats and red pants. Some had beards. Some had glasses. They all held twigs of blackthorn that looked like long wooden hammers.

Oisín grabbed Molly's leg with both hands; she put her arm around him.

"Oh, Oisín, don't be scared, they're Leprechauns! Seeing a Leprechaun is the luckiest of lucky things that can happen to you, and we've found a whole party of them. We're in Tír Na n'Óg."

"What will they do to us?" asked Oisín.

"If we don't scare them away, the Leprechauns might give us a wish. Would you like that?"

Oisín didn't answer. He couldn't take his eyes off the brightly dressed men, with their funny hats and beards. He listened to their squeaky, creaky voices and the sounds of the funny sticks as they pounded a mushroom table, trying to get a word in edgeways with each other. He watched them all tucking into plates of colcannon. Suddenly one broke into song and the others joined in, singing;

"*Dilín ó deamhas, ó deamhas; dilín ó deamhas ó dí.*"

It looked like they were having a very big party for such very small people.

From the corner of their eyes, the children spotted something moving in the shadows of the nearby bushes.

"Oh no! Look out!" Roisín cried out, seeing a huge scary figure coming towards them.

As it passed behind the bushes, they saw the dark, fearsome shape of a monster. He was huge, with a ferocious face. The holes in his nose could fit a broomstick handle. He had elephant's ears and his eyes looked like two burning coals stretched over his nose. His mouth was the most terrifying of all. It was slobbery with frothy foam dripping from it. Snarling, snapping, snorting, he stood upright and he had paws like an ape. He was covered in wiry brittle hair and sticking out of each side of his head were two big fat horns.

Molly knew it was a Fir Bolg, one of the tribes that had lived in Tír Na n'Óg long, long ago, and she remembered hearing how the bulls and cows ran and hid when they sensed a Fir Bolg coming closer.

He bellowed in a loud voice,

"L E P R E C H A U N   P I E!" as he thumped his way toward where the Leprechauns sat.

"Ohhhh! What's that?" asked Oisín as he clutched Molly's hand.

"Look out!" shouted Roisín.

The Leprechauns heard the Fir Bolg and Roisín's warning. They moved quickly, as little things do. They disappeared into hiding places deep below the ground, between the roots of the huge oak tree.

The Fir Bolg was rapidly approaching. He was furious that his plans were spoiled. Hearing him sniffing, Molly knew they were still in danger. She grabbed the children tightly and scurried round the tree to stay out of his sight. But, oh dear - Oisín tripped!

"Don't worry, Oisín" whispered Roisín, bending over to hold out her hand to him. As she did, she noticed something under a branch and pointed it out to Molly and Oisín.

"I think that's a door," she whispered. Before Molly could answer, Roisín slid down; with all her might she quickly moved the branches. Just as the Fir Bolg approached the tree, she yanked the door open and they all jumped in, slamming the door behind them and bolting it shut. They heard the sound of the Fir Bolg's big paws scraping and pounding overhead and the sniffing of his snout as he followed their scent. They crept on tiptoe, deeper and deeper inside the burrow beneath the tree.

Suddenly they were welcomed by tiny cheering voices, which sounded almost like a flock of birds. They had entered the Leprechauns home.

A courtier in a green velvet jacket came towards them and bowed. He ushered them through the crowd of other little people who gathered to see them. He led them to the main hall. There he bowed in front of the Leprechaun sitting in a large high back chair. This little fellow appeared to be someone of great importance; he wore no hat and had extra braid trimming around his waistcoat. His eyes sparkled like green emeralds.

The courtier bowed to the little man in the chair and pointing to Molly and the children he said, *"A Rí, seo iad na ndaoine mór."*

Turning to the guests he bowed again while gesturing towards the seated Leprechaun and announced;

"Tis the King of us Leprechauns befor'ye."

The King stepped towards them. Oisín thought that Roisín, Molly and himself must have looked huge to this little fellow. He's no bigger than my lunch juice carton, thought Roisín but much more colourful. He bowed to Molly and the children and thanked them for saving his people from the Giant Fir Bolg.

"Sure, we're terrible grateful to ye all!" he said, in such a little Irish voice it made the children giggle.

The little fellow bowed politely again and then rose and clapped his hands briskly together.

Immediately, Leprechauns appeared from the other end of their tree-root residence. Molly and the children had to stoop and be very careful where they put their feet, in case they might step on one of their tiny hosts.

The Leprechauns, who had been called by the King, were struggling with buckets filled with a foaming yellow liquid. They heaved them across the room and offered Molly and the children a drink.

"What is this?" asked Molly, cautiously.

"Daisy-down-dilly-lemonade, if ye please," answered the King. To the children, the Leprechaun buckets were no bigger than their smallest sand bucket.

"Why thank you most kindly, your Leprechaun Highness," she replied. Not wanting to offend him, she moved to the table where the little people had placed a tray of goblets, which were the size of her sewing thimbles. With her back to the King she separated three goblets and quickly pulled a potion from her bag and sprinkled it over them. The children smiled as they watched her.

Molly showed them how to hold the goblets gently between two fingers and take tiny sips. It would have been very impolite to drink it all at once. It tasted so refreshing; the children hoped their little thimbles would never be empty.

The Leprechauns were most welcoming and polite, keen to show the children and Molly around their humble home, deep beneath the big oak tree.

Heading further down the tunnel, coiling among the roots of the mighty oak tree they came to another long room with lots of little beds, lined along both walls. Beside each bed was a stand for their clothes, a hook for their hats and a table for their glasses.

Further along still, was a lovely sitting room with a fireplace with lots of little chairs, and musical instruments so small even the children had to squint their young eyes to make out the violins, bodhrans, fiddles, flutes, penny whistles, and spoons a-plenty, and in the corner, a tiny, beautiful harp.

The only window in the house was above this corner. It looked out on the base of the tree, allowing the sun, rainbow and moon beams to shine through. Alongside the harp was an enormous cooking pot, fat-bellied and old. Even to Molly and the children, this was a big container, bigger than the biggest pumpkin they had ever seen. It must have looked even bigger to the Little People.

Beams of light came in through the window and lit the space where the pot stood. The rays of light were different colours. First there was red, then orange, yellow, green, blue, indigo and finally, violet. They lit up the solid gold pieces bursting from the pot. It was the famous crock of gold, said to be found at the end of a rainbow, just as the children had always heard in their storybooks. And here it was beside them!

Gobsmacked, Oisín's and Roisín's mouths hung open. They had never imagined that a rainbow could come out at night. Things like that only seemed to happen when they were with Molly.

"Oh my! This is such a lovely place," said Molly. The little King was busy organizing the other Leprechauns.

"*Tar isteach,*" he uttered *"agus sui síos, más é do thoil é."*

He gave a flourish of his varnished blackthorn stick, shaped like a hammer.

Molly had told the children it was called a 'shillelagh'. That made the children think of shilly-shally, which they were always told not to do, so they giggled.

Upon the King's signal, the little musicians took their tiny seats near the fireplace, and began playing.

"*Dilín ó deamhas, ó deamhas; dilín ó deamhas ó dí,*" which definitely seemed to be the favourite song of these Little People. It was such fun. The children had never heard music so jolly or seen such wonderful, tiny dancers in all their lives.

All too soon, it was over and the little people began to yawn. It was clearly getting late.

"Why thank you kindly, sir," said Molly. "We really need to get going. It will soon be the children's bedtime."

"Do we have to go, Molly?" whinged Oisín, tugging her hand, unable to take his eyes off the little people.

"Please Molly, can we stay a little longer,

"P L E A S E?" begged Roisín.

Before she could respond, the King interrupted.

"Before ye go, children," he said in his biggest Leprechaun voice, "ye have been so good, so polite and well behaved, and aren't ye after savin' all my people from that infuriatin' awful Fir Bolg. It's my duty now to offer ye a wish. Now I'm not God Almighty and it's only a little Leprechaun I am indeed, but it's special powers I have, special enough that I can grant you your heart's desire, whatever that might be. Do ye have a wish? Ye only have to say it and I'll be grantin' it."

Roisín as the oldest child, thought she should answer.

"I beg your pardon, Mr. King of the Little People, sir, but would it be alright if I asked a question first? In fact would it be rude if I asked you two things?"

"No trouble at all, no trouble at all – ask away, ask away!" replied the King, as if he had to answer twice, maybe because there were two questions, but really just because that's how many Irish people – big or small – talk, never using only one word, when you can use two or, better still, ten.

Roisín was a little unsure over her questions, only daring to ask because her curiosity was stronger than her embarrassment.

She cleared her throat. "Well," she began, "Well sir, why is it such small people have such a huge crock of gold that everyone's always trying to find and never can? And why is it you can grant me anything I want, but you can't get rid of that horrible Fir Bolg outside?"

The King of the little people stepped back and his mouth fell open in amazement. He pulled and stroked his red beard slowly.

"Well, well, we-elll! Aren't ye the smart one!" said the King. "Indeed ye've asked it to me straight, right enough you have. And even though I'm allowed answer ye with a riddle, and even though I love riddles, I'm going to answer ye straight back and no messing' about at all, at all."

The children beamed at each other. Molly smiled and squeezed their hands.

"To your first question," said the King, "I have this to say. The reason we have so much gold is, we never use it, because we've no need for it! We have everything we need right here - a happy home, each other, music, stories, dancing' and all the love in the world. An' the only reason you found that crock of gold is you were too busy enjoying yourselves being children to be bothered looking for it."

He stepped closer. "You see nobody who goes looking for it ever finds it. It's yours by the way, that's the rule, finders keepers. But let me give ye some good advice. You'd be better to just leave that old crock just where it is. There's no good will ever come of having it and you're such nice children. But take it with my blessing' if that's what ye want, but better ye take my advice. I wouldn't wish it on the old' Fir Bolg out there and that's straight up, me little darlings!"

Roisín was staring at him. She could hardly believe her ears.

"People are forever coming looking for the gold," he continued. "They've forgotten about the magic and about us, but they never forget the crock o'gold. It brings bad company. People that wouldn't sit to tea with a man, and people a man wouldn't drink porter with. It's bad luck and that's the truth of it."

The other Leprechauns stared at Molly and the children as their King continued.

"Which brings me to your second question. We can't get rid of the big old Fir Bolg because it would take a magic spell or somebody mighty strong and clever to trap him. Now we're peace loving people, and bad as he is, we've no desire to do him any harm and make ourselves just like him. And though we can grant other people's wishes, we can't grant wishes to ourselves. So we're kind of stuck with him. Does that answer your question?"

The little King stood with one hand leaning on his shillelagh and the other pulling at his long, red beard. He was staring at Roisín, curious to hear her wish.

She could feel his eyes on her; indeed, everybody's eyes were on her – Molly's, Oisín's and all the Little People's.

At last she spoke,

"Alright, I know what I want – what we all want, Molly, Oisín and me."

"And what might that be?" asked the King.

Roisín spoke loudly for everyone in the room to hear.

"I wish the huge Fir Bolg would go away and take the crock of gold with him, forever and ever and ever. Then people will have to look for the gold where the horrible Fir Bolg is and stop bothering you and the lovely Little People all the time."

She hesitated. "Can you do that, sir?"

Suddenly, without there being anyone anywhere near it, the harp beside the crock of gold played a beautiful, lilting melody of notes, and the crock of gold vanished.

At that moment, the Fir Bolg howled outside the hidden door. The pot had crashed against his head as it shot up from the tree. He was angry.

"What was that?" he yelled, jumping up. But as soon as he spotted the crock of gold he roared with joy. His howl faded quickly into the far, far distance, over the hills and far away – never, never to return.

The Little People danced and sang and twirled each other about in a merry dance that the Irish people – big and small – call a jig.

The little King was only able to hug two fingers of Roisín's right hand but he hugged them as tight as ever a Leprechaun could hug, and there were tears of joy in his tiny emerald eyes. It was time to go.

Oisín began pulling and tugging at Molly's hand.

"What is it?" she asked.

"How come I never got a wish?" he asked, stamping his foot on the ground.

"We all got our wish Oisín," she replied

As they were about to leave the tree house, the King handed each one of them a shillelagh, saying;

"Our thanks and the blessings of the trees be with ye all, always."

Oisín was thrilled; he couldn't wait to show it to his friends.

Outside the moon was still beaming, and that's how it was in Tír Na n'Óg, *fadó, fadó, fadó*. Molly touched her magic brooch and uttered her special words *"Trasna na dtonnta"*. In seconds they were whooshed back across the ocean, safely onto their couch.

"Open your eyes now children. The rain has stopped. We need to take a walk and get some fresh air. We've been inside all day," said Nan.

"We weren't inside," cried Oisín, "we were with Molly at the little people's house under the tree."

"And my wish was to get rid of an old hairy monster," piped Roisín, "the little people had a band and everything!"

"Sounds delightful," said Nan, "I must have dozed off."

The children looked at each other and Nan in wonderment. Then Oisín picked up a shillelagh by the couch "Look what I got!" he said as he marched off to show his friends.

Translations

(1)   *Trasna na dtonnta, dul shiar dul shiar* : Over the waves and far away

(2)   *Tír Na n'Óg* : Land of youth.

(3)   *Fa-dó fa-dó fa-dó* : Long. long ago.

(4)   *Dilín ó deamhas, ó deamhas; dilín ó deamhas, ó dí:*
      From an Irish children's dance verse.

(5)   *Tar isteach* : Come in.

(6)   *Agus sui sios, más é do thoil é* : And sit down, if you please

(7)   *Shillelagh* : small hawthorn stick, looks like a crooked hammer

(8)   *Bodhran* : Irish small hand drum

(9)   *Colcannon* : mashed potatoes mixed with onions and cabbage

(10) *A Rí, seo iad na ndaoine mór* : My King these are the big people.

Caitriona Stewart Short

Leaving Belfast, 1941

You wouldn't have known that there was a war on because it seemed most of the population of Belfast had turned up at the Great Northern Railway to take the train to Dublin. Passengers were milling around the long marble platforms waiting for the guard to announce boarding time, and groups of excited people were throwing rice and confetti at the newly married couple bound for their honeymoon in a boarding house in Drumcondra.

The big metal giant of a train hissed and seethed out clouds of steam up into the Victorian rafters of the station, unsettling families of resident pigeons. The guard blew his whistle, the long noisy blast screeched through the air:

"All aboard! All aboard! All passengers bound for Amiens Street, Dublin! All aboard!"

Simultaneously the great train expelled a thunderous belch of steam; a cheering crowd carried the newly-weds shoulder-high to their carriage, and then through the steaming, whistling, whooping crowd emerged a small platoon of cyclists, the Belfast Cycling Club, khaki-clad in shorts, with knapsacks on their backs and strong boots on their feet.

They swung their bicycles high over their shoulders, up and over into the mail carriage with the enthusiasm and energy of the young in summer and the heady carefree liberating uncertainty of wartime – this was the start of their great expedition, cycling around the Irish coastline in two weeks.

"Do you think that she'll turn up, Jackie?"

"Yeah, of course she will. Sure didn't I ask her to marry me last week?"

Hand in hand, a young brother and sister stood back from the throng on the platform, their backs pressed up against the thick marble columns, with their gas masks strung bandolier-style across their chests and each bearing a label announcing to all that they were called James and Sadie. A man in a uniform guided them on to the train to make the long journey to Dublin to stay with the Auntie Ginney they had never met.

Then, running through the thronging, waving crowds came the young Ellie.

"I'm here, I'm here! Don't go without me!" she called out to the smiling faces hanging out of the carriage windows.

Ellie climbed on to the train, wearing khaki shorts, but rolled up thigh-high, shirt tucked tight into her waist, a headscarf tied up into a turban like Gloria Swanson and red high heels on her feet like Betty Grable.

"Hey Jackie, she'll not do much cycling wearing that outfit."

"Ah, she'll do all right, sure didn't I buy a tandem bicycle so she wouldn't get lost!"

The guard gave a long warbling blow on his whistle: carriage doors were slammed shut; the Great Northern train lurched and heaved forward; it clanked and rattled, then paused and shuddered. Gathering its energy it puffed a rumble of steam down the length of the platform, then travelled upwards into the echoing steel rafters.

A swoop of pigeons took flight, up into the hazy sun streams filtering in through the glass-panelled roof, the newly-weds waved out from their window, well wishers cheered and shouted:

"Don't be doing anything that I wouldn't do!"

"Aye and bring us back some butter from the Free State!"

Caitriona Stewart Short

The Postman

The postman trundled up the long driveway to the villa on his old Vespa scooter. It crackled and backfired into the warm morning air. He wore his official cap at a jaunty angle and his bag of deliveries was strung bandolier-style over his chest. Avoiding the large potholes in the ground, he gave a few extra revs on the throttle. The Vespa responded obligingly and raised its whining engine up a few decibels.

Foto, the resident stray dog, burst through the hydrangea bushes yapping and barking; the back wheel kicked up stony gravel and the smell of two-stroke fumed the air. Juan made the final sprint up the slight incline of the driveway, closely pursued by Foto, and arrived abruptly at the front door of the villa, in balloons of dust clouds.

Foto recognised his adversary and jumped and snapped at his heels; he knew what to expect.

"So, my little friend, have they fed you today?"

Juan opened his postbag and rummaged into its depths. Foto sprang into the air, twisting and turning in figures of eight, yelping and yowling but never taking his gaze from the bag.

"Yes, I have brought something for you, here we are."

Juan produced a small paper parcel. He unwrapped it and set down the bone he had brought from Carlos the butcher's shop.

"Tell me, Foto, how is it that a man who does not live all the time here at Villa Lorenzo, gets so much mail very week?"

The Villa was on his postal route, and when Senora Delia had lived there, she had a post box installed at the gateway down at the entrance on the road.

Of course Senora Delia was a very private person and only received correspondence from her solicitor in Madrid, or very infrequently, from her son in New York, however it meant that Juan didn't have to make the detour up the long driveway to the front door. This had been very convenient for him because he could be back at his house to have coffee on the terrace with his wife Dolores and then go off to tend his bees. Now it was most inconvenient indeed for Juan, this detour added another fifteen minutes on to his round and he would be late for lunch at the café.

He took out the bundle of letters which had been tied together with large, thick elastic bands.

"Hah," he muttered in disgust, "these will not fit into the letterbox; I will have to go around to the back and leave them in the basket at the kitchen door."

Juan walked around the side of the house, through the scented arch of bougainvillea and into the parterre herb garden. He deposited the package in the large wicker basket outside the long windowed kitchen door. Nardilla's handiwork was clear to be seen all around. The terrace had been swept and the garden furniture arranged to take full advantage of the views down the valley. Tall and small ceramic pots had been planted with early summer flowers and arranged in clusters of colours and smells. However there was no sign of Nardilla.

"Imagine that – having a housekeeper to keep a house with no one living in it?" he asked the little Jack Russell who had followed behind him, carrying his bone. He sat down at Juan's feet and then out of appreciation of his trusty friend, he lifted his hind leg and piddled on his boots.

"Ah! Little bastard." Juan lifted his slightly wet boot and sent it in the dog's direction but Foto was too quick for him, he had already darted off into the bushes with his treasure to bury it in his secret place.

"Well, he must have a lot of money to spend, a big empty house, lots of letters and no one here to read them. Now Foto I must be off, I am already late for my bees," he called over his shoulder. The crack and backfire of the scooter's ignition echoed through the still air; Foto sprang out of the lavender bushes and barked the scooter all the way to the entrance gate.

Since his beloved wife, Dolores, had died last year, Juan had continued with his daily routine. He would rise early in the morning after six and attend to his small farm chores; he had kept Dolores' clutter of hens, geese and ducks and continued to sell them and their eggs at the nearby weekly market in Solado. Then at eight o'clock he would go off on his postal round - a twenty kilometre ride.

Of course he had his usual stops along the way: Senor Alvarez, the retired college professor from Sevilla, a keen bee-keeper, he and the professor would exchange details about their hives and take coffee at his kitchen table; then there was Xavier and his busy wife, Altara, who were artisan cheese makers – naturally he would congratulate them on the excellence of their cheeses, and they in turn would insist that he join them in a small plate of tapas and a little wine to fortify him on his rounds. He tried to avoid spending too much time with Senora Manila. She was twice widowed and rumour had it that she was on the look out for another husband, so he usually declined to take coffee or tapas but would sometimes, reluctantly, accept a warm roll of her bread wrapped in a spotless tea towel.

Throughout his thirty years marriage to Dolores they had moulded into a comfortable routine. Dolores would always insist on setting the table for lunch. In winter, on the long kitchen table beside the big range and in summer, on the wide open terrace. She especially liked the summer dining table. It had been a wedding present from her three brothers and was carved and honed from a cedar wood tree on the family farm. It came with eight comfortable high backed chairs. It was her custom to have lunch prepared for twelve thirty, and sometimes Juan would arrive with his neighbours, the Delanos from the nearby vineyard – so she always liked to be prepared and have plenty of food for unexpected guests.

The midday meal was prepared in the shade of the terrace: her seasonal house speciality, wild boar, which Juan and Carlos had shot themselves, was slowly cooking in wild garlic and juniper berries on the summer hob; courgettes, aubergines, vine tomatoes and shallots were roasting on the open barbeque; a large bowl of cool summer leaves stood waiting to be drizzled in Dolores' home pressed olive oil and her warm corn bread was wrapped in a tea towel ready for eating. The wine was resting – it had been a good year.

It was on such a warm Autumn day in late September, that the tranquillity of the midday sojourn was cracked by the familiar backfire of Juan's Vespa. It had become his calling card and immediately alerted Pepe, their old sheepdog, who would slowly raise himself up from his nook under Juan's chair on the terrace and amble to the edge of the shade. Here he would settle down and wait for Juan.

Parp! Parp! Parp! Parp! He tooted on his horn, as he puttered to a halt at the kitchen door beside the terrace.

"Dolores, Dolores, I am here! What do you think? The foreigner has returned to Villa Lorenzo."

But today Pepe was not there. By the time Juan was standing on his summer terrace, he knew that Dolores had not stirred from her chair. She was still warm to the touch, he had just missed her.

Juan sat down at her feet and rested himself against her knees; Pepe whined and whimpered from his hiding place under the chair. He removed his cap out of respect and buried his face in his rough brown hands; he sighed and then cried loudly, longingly and mournfully.

The evening sun had moved across the terrace leaving the long summer table in shadow. Juan was now still and silent; Dolores sat in repose in her chair, her face resting and glowing in the warmth of the Autumn sun.

Caitriona Stewart Short

Frankie and Amelia

Frankie leaned against the bar and ordered a drink.

"Usual for me, Samos."

"Coming up, Mr. Frankie. Campari and ice, with a slice of orange, just as you like it."

Frankie walked out to the small terrace. The afternoon sun hit his face like a furnace fire. Even after all these years he found the heat unbearable in August. He put on his sunglasses and took up his usual seat at the corner table, in the shade of the awning.

Taverna Samos was carved into the crook of the mountain between the sea and the long, steep climb up to the monastery at its summit. Frankie looked out over the sea and down to the sheltered harbour below. The view from Samos' café bar over the Mediterranean had been the enduring and inspiring reason for him to remain on the island: the wide blue sea painted itself into the horizon of the summer sky, the white light of the sun by day mellowed into the orange red glow of the evening.

Gulls screeched and swooped high and low over a fishing boat as it glided homeward on smooth calm waters; the passenger ferry came into view, rounding the headland, visibly lilting and heaving with day - trippers and tourists. He observed Georgios the fishmonger, in his white pick up van as it wended its precarious way down the hillside to meet the boats. By the time he reached the harbour, the men were already unloading their catch. He recognised a small group of local restaurant owners inspecting boxes of fish, their arms waving in the air, bartering for the best prices. Seabirds squawked and hovered in the air waiting their opportunity.

This was his piece of heaven. This was where he had been sitting when he had first meet Amelia.

Samos emerged from the dark, cool, cavern of the café. He walked with a slight hurry to his step: rotund, but neat and gracious in his gait, he served the drinks from a large tray balanced on the upturned fingers of his hand.

Elegantly, he bowed from the waist to deliver the tall glass of cherry-coloured liquor to the table.

"Here we are Mr. Frankie, Campari. It is another beautiful day to admire the view?"

"As always, Samos, as always. Any news of your niece in London?"

"Not yet – but we cannot hurry the birth of a new baby, can we Mr. Frankie?"

The Campari was accompanied by a small carafe of water and a glass dish with two ice cubes and a pair of tongs and, as he spoke, Samos arranged these with understated precision on the marble topped table. Clearly his years as a Head Waiter and then Maitre D in some of the best hotels in London would not be compromised in his café.

"Thanks, *ephkharisto*, Samos."

"As always, it is my pleasure, Mr. Frankie."

Satisfied with his service, Samos placed the large serving tray under his arm. He bowed and then retreated into his café.

Frankie sipped the cool, dry drink, lit up a small cigar and inhaled the sweet tobacco. This was the view that had brought him here, the view he remembered from London, the view in the battered picture on the wall of a small Greek restaurant down the old Kent Road, where he grew up.

The proprietor, Mrs. Stephanos, would lovingly polish the picture of her family view and sometimes she would stare into the hillside village and quietly talk to the man in the yellow shirt sitting outside its café. Then there were the days when her dark-skinned, bulky arms would vigorously rub into the depths of its wide blue sea, bringing a sweat to her wrinkled brow: she would lapse into her village dialect and berate the fishermen in their small boats, hauling in their catch of fish.

"Where are the fresh sardines in London, eh?"

Yes, thought Frankie, this is the place. Strange though, that I should end up here, in this village, living in Mrs. Stephanos' picture. But today was the day that he had arranged to meet Amelia. He wondered if she would come.

Tom Barrett

Bee Navigation

The *Evening Herald* suddenly appeared on my desk, placed there by my son-in-law. "Tom," he said, "You have been talking about keeping bees for years, now you can do something about it." I looked at the advertisement placed there by the County Dublin Beekeeping Association, detailing practical lessons for beginners in beekeeping. A short phone call later and I was enrolled in the course. My foot was firmly on the first rung of the beekeeping ladder, a ladder which led me to a hobby which I have found both interesting and rewarding. That was twelve years ago.

Billy Mellon was a wonderful instructor in the craft of beekeeping. It seems that there was hardly ever a time during his long sojourn on the planet when he was not a beekeeper. If there was, Billy could not remember it. His brilliance in beekeeping was matched with a consummate skill in teaching the subject. Sadly, Billy is no longer with us.

Our instructor explained, in detail, the theory of the subject, describing to a hushed audience the life cycle of the bees and where they fit in the natural order. The queen's role in the scheme of things enthralled the listeners, even more so when we saw her in action during the practical demonstrations in the apiary in Rathfarnham. It was during one of these demonstrations that we saw several bees carrying out what Billy described as the 'Waggle Dance' on the honeycombs. My interest in Bee Navigation was born.

The Global Positioning System – GPS – was at that time in its earliest stages and already I had seen a beekeeper with a clever gismo which could tell him where he was on the planet to within a few metres. I thought, "This is clever stuff - it sure improves on the old system of triangulation and bench marks in use for centuries." The GPS system required the use of satellites in orbit around the earth at huge expense, yet this was progress and we sure liked it. Consulting signposts and stopping another human to enquire where we were was rapidly becoming a thing of the past.

As the beekeeping course proceeded, it became very evident that the bee is a very clever insect indeed. It knows the position of its hive to within ten centimeters as can be easily seen if a hive is moved. Returning bees will come back to the old position of the hive, fly in circles as though stacked at Heathrow and then reprogramme their Navigation System until they find the hive. GPS compares poorly with bee navigation, accurate within only metres, to the bees' centimeters, and the bees have not yet learned the science of rockets to launch orbiting satellites. But then they do not need to!

The bee's ability to lead an efficient life is quite remarkable, and this is probably best illustrated in its skill in locating sources of nectar and pollen. We listened with bated breath as Billy explained, at the open hive in Rathfarnham, how the Waggle Dance operates. When a bee locates a good source of forage it collects nectar and brings it back to the hive. It then does a figure-of-eight dance on the comb, such that the orientation of the figure-of-eight indicates the direction of the forage, relative to the position of the sun. The number of times per second which the dancing bee waggles indicates the distance from the hive to the forage – which humans then translate into miles or kilometers. The bee needs no such translation. The direction of the bee's movements represents either towards or away from the sun. A sample of the forage is then passed to the bees waiting in a circle around the dancer. Thus each of the observing bees now knows what forage is available and its direction and its distance from the hive. But it has been noted by humans that the observing bees do not necessarily leave the hive immediately after the dance has ended, which generates a complication.

We all know that the apparent position of the sun in the sky changes at 15 degrees per hour or a degree of arc every four minutes. And it is changing while the bee is flying to the forage. Both of these variables must be taken into account by the bee on its way to the forage and its flight path must be adjusted accordingly. "By marking bees and placing human observers at the site of the forage we have proved that all of this happens," declared Billy, with a visible sense of pride in these tiny navigators. And no bee has ever heard of a degree of arc or a mile or a kilometer, nor had access to mathematics or computers. They have been carrying out this remarkable feat of navigation since they first appeared on the planet over thirty million years ago, millions of years before humans.

"But," asked one of the student beekeepers, "suppose that it is a dull day and the bees cannot see the sun, what then?" The bees had the answer to that one too. They see using ultra-violet light, so they can always see the sun. Billy was in full flight at this lecture!

But our instructor had not finished his lecture on navigation yet. A diagram of a high mountain with a beehive on one side of it, and containers of sugar syrup on the far side of the mountain was placed on the board. Billy went on to recount a truly remarkable experiment on bee navigation carried out in Germany many years before. This was known as the Schafberg experiment, named after the mountain.

The only source of food for a colony of bees was put on the far side of a mountain diametrically opposite the hive. The bees could not fly over the mountain, only around it. What direction would the bees indicate in their dancing? The answer was surprising; the bees indicated the direction through the mountain at an angle they could obviously not fly. The distance indication however, was for the long flight around the mountain. Bees marked by the beekeepers duly arrived at the forage having carried out calculations which would require humans to use advanced mathematics and navigation equipment.

Or do the bees do it by calculation? Just because this is how we would have to do it is no reason for believing that this is how the bees do it. The truth is that we will probably never know, but it is difficult not to have a sneaking suspicion that they have learned something during their thirty million years on the planet that we do not know.

But if we wish to learn the secrets of bee navigation we had better move quickly. Latest reports from beekeeping scientists indicate, that if the present rate of bee loss continues, the marvellous insect has in the region of ten years left on the planet. Human greed, stupidity and pressure on the environment, caused by burgeoning human numbers and life style, has generated a lethal cocktail of agricultural poisons which is proving fatal to the bees and, indeed, to everything else.

Billions of bees are now dying each year. Many scientists are of the opinion that these poisons are compromising the bees' superb navigation system, causing them to fail to return to their hives. And when the last honeybee dies, its secrets die with it. A species with less than a million years on the planet is destroying a species with thirty million years clocked up; nay, it is now destroying the entire surface of the earth itself.

Enough said!

Tom Barrett

A Train Journey in Corsica

We slept well on the ferry from Toulon on its twelve hour overnight journey to Corsica. A knock on the cabin door at 6.00 am announced that the Corsican port of Bastia was just one hour away so we arose to prepare ourselves for disembarkation. A warning that there would be heavy rain in Bastia was not well received, but I suppose that Irish people are more used to rain than most.

The aroma of freshly brewed coffee, which I always associate with France, wafted towards us as we joined a queue of some eager and some weary passengers waiting for breakfast. After a quick breakfast of cereal and coffee we joined the other '*pietons*' – foot passengers – waiting for the ship to come along side. They were right about the rain and we were wrong about the Irish being used to it. This rain was falling in sheets; it was almost like standing under a waterfall. Having left the ferry we met two Dublin men joining the ship on their way back to Ireland after a mountaineering holiday. "You will enjoy the island," was their parting shot, as they joined the queue for the ferry. Not a cab was to be seen, so we donned our waterproof clothing and headed out on foot for the station, which we reached in about 15 minutes. On the way, we were at times drenched by the fast moving cars throwing up masses of water, which was gathering from the downpour. Eventually a small quiet little station greeted us, with the familiar clock tower beloved of the designers of many French railway stations.

The interior of the station was bright and cheerful. A backpacking passenger laden with luggage sat a few metres from us taking an occasional swig from his large bottle of water, a woman with two children sat on the far side of us, the children delighting in running around the floor, being occasionally admonished by an increasingly exasperated mother. A small queue had formed for the ticket office; a young, pleasant lady sold us the tickets and confirmed the train times, as we then waited on not too comfortable seats for the train to arrive.

Just five minutes before departure the train pulled in and we began boarding. The woman with the two children rounded up her charges, the backpacker rounded up his luggage, other passengers who had cut it fine hurried in through the doors. Some people will always cut things fine. A businessman – the best dressed passenger in the station, complete with brief case and laptop – joined the throng for the train. Ten minutes later, with a loud blast, the train moved off on our three and three quarter hour journey to Ajaccio, the island capital.

The interior of the train was comfortable but a little sparse. The seats lacked the luxury of the modern train, but this was part of its charm. Were we not travelling in Corsica and did we not expect things to be charmingly different? The quiet sounds of French were music to our ears as I take every opportunity to listen to this beautiful language whenever I can. The advertisements, of course in French, were otherwise no different to those seen elsewhere. The businessman with his laptop on his knees was busying himself, presumably for a meeting in Ajaccio. Funny, the mixture of a laptop linked to the Internet on an old train on a faraway island. A young boy fiddled with a Playstation or other device. Some conversations were being carried out on the ubiquitous mobile. But lacking on this journey was the pungent smell of the Gitane cigarettes so beloved of the French in days gone by; smoking is now forbidden on all French trains – even on the remote island of Corsica.

Immediately after pulling out, we enter the first of a great many tunnels, tunnels cut through the mountainous country which is the island of Corsica. Some of these tunnels are immensely long by comparison to say those in Wales, the train travelling quite slowly but appearing to travel at high speed due to the nearness of the tunnel walls.

The sea is now on our left as the train sways around bends which come in quick succession. The man with the laptop is grabbing his PC to prevent it from falling as the train heaves around some sharp bends. We have just passed an Evangelical Church at Furiani station, where the train stopped for barely a minute. Plenty of trees can be seen, this island is still extensively wooded. The occasional farmhouse appears and, just as promptly, disappears in what seems to be a sparsely populated area. A tractor is working in the field below us as we look into a large valley surrounded by high mountains.

The heavy rain which greeted us on arrival is now just an Irish mist, and the day is brightening up considerably. We get talking to a Corsican passenger who explained that the weather in the mountains is subject to sudden change. I always find it exciting speaking in French and trying to listen intently to pick up what is being said at the high speed at which the French converse. Of course I ask him – as always – to please slow down a bit, which he does for a minute or two and then resumes his high speed delivery. At 8.55 am we are at Biguglia, seven minutes late according to the timetable. Eight minutes later we arrive at Borgo and a further ten minutes brings us to Casamozza; a big station by comparison to what we have seen yet.

Some extra passengers join the train, which is still far from full. The backpacker is a few seats away from us, busily eating a rather large piece of French bread with what appears to be salami. The smell of garlic is beginning to assail our nostrils, a smell which we do not find unpleasant. The train suffers from draughts – or rather we do – so we pull our now dry waterproof clothing around us. The laptop man is still working away, he has probably seen this lovely scenery so many times that it is now of little interest to him.

Corsica has had a very exciting history, having been run by Italian towns like Pisa and Genoa, but of course it is now part of France. Indeed one of its most famous sons, Napoleon Bonaparte, was born in Ajaccio, to which we are travelling. French is the main language of the island but Corsican, which is a derivative of Italian, is also spoken.

This train journey is the most spectacular I have ever been on. A large olive grove is now visible below us, high mountains are in the distance as the train slows and seems to be labouring under the strain of the ascent, as the mountains come ever nearer. A huge valley is now below us as we see the road snaking around the mountains with a few cars visible. Driving on these roads must be very demanding.

High peaks now tower above us. The train enters and leaves tunnels in rapid succession as we travel deeper and deeper into the middle of the island. A wide stream full of rocks is now rushing towards the ocean. Little evidence of human habitation can be seen. These are inhospitable mountains, home to wild boar, birds of prey and many small furry animals - birds can be seen in profusion. Nature seems to reign supreme in the middle of Corsica, safe from the marauding attention of Homo sapiens. What a vista now presents itself – very high mountains and deep valleys – we are probably only half way up the mountains. We see a great many streams flowing rapidly and sometimes a placid river, interspersed with waterfalls.

A few feet from us, with a loud thud, the backpacks and other baggage owned by our backpacker tumble from the luggage rack as the train rounds one of the bends, spilling baggage all over the floor. Our backpacking passenger interrupts his meal to push the luggage back on to the rack. Two other tourists are in animated conversation as the magnificent scenery unfolds like watching a travel film.

That Corsican who spoke of sudden weather changes was, I fear, quite right, heavy rain is now obscuring our view of these dazzling mountains, as the train pulls into Ponte Nuovo at 9.30 am, only three minutes late. Magnificent country for rock climbing is now to our right, solid rock with the odd pocket of vegetation, sheer cliff faces with lumps of rock jutting out almost touching the train. We have now come out of an exceptionally long tunnel and suddenly the countryside has changed. This is an area of lush wild vegetation; hardly a rock is to be seen. A farmhouse comes into view with its vineyard. Corsican wines, mostly rosé, have a good reputation and we can attest to the accuracy of this.

The train is now standing in Ponto Lecchio, the main junction on the island. All trains from Calvi and Ile Rousse in the North West to Bastia in the North East and Ajaccio in the west pass through Ponto Lecchio. Heavy rain continues to fall as we continue on our journey.

At the halfway mark we enter Corte. We are now looking down on the peaks we were looking up at only an hour before, or so it seemed to me. These mountains look as if they go on forever, but maybe it is just that I want them to! A large group of bikers now join the train, complete with bicycles and rucksacks piled in a disorganised heap at the back of our carriage.

And now the descent begins with frequent screeching of brakes; until eventually we are in flat country for the last few kilometres to Ajaccio. The rain clouds are now gone and bright sunshine greets us as we slowly pull into the station. The mountains, over which we have just travelled, now stand like distant sentinels watching over the capital, their lofty peaks in the clouds. I have tried to capture some of that thrilling journey on film and in my notebook, but there is no substitute for being there. I would hope some day to go back to Corsica, *Ile de Beaute* as it is called by the French, and deservedly so.

Declan Houton

Pay Rise

The stuff Enda says never fails to amaze us,
Of his latest attack, I just thought, "Ah Jay-sus,"
You'd tink I'm the only one here getting raises,
But I just want to get what I'm due.

Those muppets are mad 'cos I got more than they did,
The hounds from the press will be frothin' and rabid,
I'll keep me head down for a few weeks and stay hid,
And then I will take what I'm due.

Me fellow world leaders are all very cosy,
In Chequers, Camp David, sure everyting's rosy,
There's even a palace for that guy Sarkozy,
Don't tell me that's more than I'm due.

An' everyone tinks that it's easy being me,
They don't realise, I don't get tings for free,
They quickly mount up you know, those cups of tea,
Oh yes, I will get what I'm due.

It seems while this pay rise is perfectly sound,
It can wait till the country's on more stable ground,
And so in the meantime I'll have a whip-round,
A dig-out . . . till I get my due.

Declan Houton

Her

When the total is more than the sum of the parts,
When a debit increases the principal,
I know deep inside of my own heart of hearts,
That love may be blind but not sensible.

I can't calculate all the blessings bestowed,
The computer's not yet been invented.
Till eternity comes I will pay what is owed,
But my huge debt won't even be dented.

Because so much is taken for granted by me,
As my life rushes by in a blur.
I can't put a value on my mortal time,
And it's thanks to my memories of her.

Declan Houton

Circling

Birds' skulls bleaching in the sunset,
stillness lurking at the end of day,
shadows creep along the bones
whose only future is decay.

Once they flew closer to the sun,
free to swoop and soar at will,
now they are anchored to the ground,
where they will settle, cold and still.

As they return to mother earth
and nourish her as those gone by,
they'll live again in those who feed
and so perhaps will never die.

Declan Houton

The Wardrobe Monster

There's a Monster in my wardrobe, that no-one else can see,
They don't believe me – Mum & Dad – 'cos he only comes at me.
When they've tucked me up at night, and I've said all my prayers,
The Monster will be glaring down, before they've reached the stairs.

They leave the night-light on for me, but Monster doesn't care,
And even when I close my eyes, I feel his deathly stare.
He's always in the second door, it's closer to my bed,
I really hate you Monster, and I wish that you were dead.

The tree outside my window, is the Monster's loyal friend,
He's like a lookout in the wind, when he starts to bend.
He watches both my parents, when they're looking at TV,
And taps upon my window if they're coming up to me.

I scrunch up to the pillow, in case he reaches out,
I'm ready with my loudest voice, in case I have to shout.
My Mum will be here in a flash, I've told him so before,
But in case he has forgotten, I tell him just once more.

My heart is beating loudly now, it sounds just like my drum,
My Daddy only laughs at me, I hope he doesn't come.
Perhaps my Mom will visit me, and help me count the sheep,
She might even read a story, until I go to sleep.

I must stay ready with my shout – I stop myself from yawning,
But sometime I will fall asleep, and wake up in the morning.
All day I can forget him, until my prayers' "Amen,"
And then I will be left alone, to face him once again.

Declan Houton
Dark Night

eyes adjust to
earthly light

a false dawn

human outlines
exchange muffled sounds

sinking realisation
anger
guilt

no chill of death
but burning shame

sleep
I was only asleep

time to face the music.

Vista 210 x 150mm *mixed media on panel*   © Padhraig Nolan 2008   www.padhraignolan.com

padhraig@padhraignolan.com

Declan Houton

Adam & Eve

Before the year dot,
When God had a lot,
Of what we call 'time' on His hands,
He thought He'd create,
A man and his mate,
And so issued some godly commands.

God spoke to the man,
And told him His plan,
How 'woman' would be really great.
The man dived right in,
"Make her tall, make her thin."
God was getting quite close to irate.

God said "It's too much,
You want such n' such,
Get up, this is no time to beg.
It will be quite a task,
But I'll grant what you ask,
Though I must charge an arm and a leg."

"Oh God, just slow down,"
Said the man with a frown,
"I don't mean to moan and to crib.
I just want a chum,
With whom to have fun,
Say! What could you do for a rib?"

cont'd >>

And when it was done,
God asked man to come,
To see what He'd made from his side.
The man he was pleased,
His chores would be eased,
"I'll take her and call her my bride."

God said "Take my creation,
Without trepidation,
Over it all, you shall rule.
Except for this tree,
It is not for thee,
Its fruits are to make apple fool."

They had everything,
Except, of course sin,
And the free-will to do as they wished.
They ruled - King and Queen,
Over everything seen,
The animals, birds and the fish.

The two were so cosy,
And everything rosy,
In their Garden of Eden that day.
Then along came a snake,
With trouble to make,
And two victims to be lead astray.

The juicy red meal,
Held too much appeal,
The juice trickled down each one's face.
How those faces burned,
When their God returned,
And threw them both out in disgrace.

God suffers dismay,
To this very day,
One thing, and they just couldn't leave it,
It beggars belief,
Why they courted such grief,
He just couldn't Adam an' Eve it!

John Piggott

Crossroads

My home town, Dun Laoghaire is trapped between the sea and a low ridge that lies inland toward the mountains. Rochestown Avenue runs arrow straight along that ridge until it comes to the crossroads called Baker's Corner. I stand at that crossroads.

I have walked up from the cemetery that lies half a mile away, below us on the south side of the ridge. I say 'walked', but since my crossing over I no longer walk. I simply move, transport. I will it and it happens.

Here, now, at the crossroads, the traffic and the people come and go and move about me as they did when I was among the living. They are unaware of me, and I am increasingly oblivious to them for they do not glow as I do. Their light is buried deep within themselves. For now.

I stand on the precise geometric epicentre of this junction. This is not a matter of calculation or geometric precision. I have never been interested in, or capable of such technical craft. It is a matter of simply knowing, as surely as the foot of an athlete knows how to fall or a heart knows how and when to beat. There is a way of things which I realise now I have always known - but only now understand. Like for instance, that this crossroads is not merely an intersection, but a cosmic power point. The roads did not arrive here and intersect randomly. No. The roads were drawn to this place which now emanates its energy out along them and back into the world, into the ether.

I am looking west along Abbey Road towards the City, but I am not drawn to that place, quite the opposite. The bustle and confusion of humanity, packed in so tight there, drags and draws on my being like a weight. I turn left looking down Kill Lane toward the mountains in the south. They are beautiful and I feel them, their magnetism, their call. But I turn again, another ninety degrees to look east along Rochestown Avenue and my home. I know there is no going back. I rotate once more.

North along Kill Lane lies the town, the port and the sea. North. It must be North. I begin to move.

I gather speed quickly. I do not so much rise into the air as watch the ground fall away below me. My course is straight, level, direct, perfect. The downhill below is gentle but this level course of mine has seen me easily clear the tall tower in the fire station yard and the church steeples beyond it. Soon the boats in the harbour are small in the water now directly below. But distance, speed, even time has little meaning to me now.

Randomly, I choose a small sailboat moored at the marina. Instantly I am not merely aboard the yacht, I am the vessel itself. I can feel its buoyancy and the kiss of the salt water wrapping around my hull. I am aware of a tiny mollusc attaching its being to my own. I feel my isolation but also my attachment to the other craft on the water, my connection to them. It seems totally natural to do so. I take my leave, resuming my journey.

It is as if I never altered course or dallied with the skiff. My course has taken me almost right across to Howth Head, the high hill at the end of the peninsula which forms the bay. My speed is phenomenal now, my movement still linear, level, unflinching. A collision with this landmass is inevitable: and yet not. A thought, a wish and I would be over it, around it - whatever. But I will take no evasive action. There is simply nothing to fear.

There is no impact, no physical contact at all when I make landfall: only darkness, like when you drive into a tunnel. I know my speed has not diminished, that in fact I continue to accelerate. I sense the pull of Mother Earth, her weight, her timelessness and her gravity. While I am one with her this way, I feel cradled, warm, anchored, secure. Yet I have no desire to linger here.

I burst through into the daylight on the other side of the hill and continue to accelerate to even more fantastic speeds out over the Irish Sea. I am travelling along a perfect line, a line of longitude: but it is more than that. It is a line of power and of destiny somehow. I can feel my destination as surely as a climber feels the anchor point at the end of his rope. I know I could be there instantly. But for now I am enjoying the ride.

The last thing I am aware of as the landmass of Ireland fades behind me are emanations from the hexagonal rock formations at The Giant's Causeway on her northern coast. They speak to me of ancient visitors, of the digital core of existence but their message is not like a code, more like music: beautiful music. I carry it with me, outward on my voyage.

The ocean seems endless, even at this incredible speed. I am tempted to 'fast-forward' now toward my destination. Yet no sooner have I contemplated this than I feel drawn to the water as if it had somehow heard my thoughts and was calling me to set them aside. And instantly I am traveling below the waves.

The sensation is staggering. I have to slow down; not because of any physical law, simply because it seems inconceivable that I would pass through such beauty and not linger to savour it.

Since my crossing over, I have ceased to experience things through physical sensation. There are no feelings like smells, tastes or sounds, only the emotions they arouse; and that emotion is everywhere and I am drawn to it, wherever it lives. The more strongly it burns, the more powerfully I am drawn.

The ocean I experience now is not cold; it is not warm, it is not wet. There are no sounds, there is no silence; no dark, no light. But it is filled with emotions. They move here like great schools of fish or the other physical beings that inhabit the physical world. Immersed in this medium, these feelings can be transmitted over great distances it seems, and with an intensity I can almost feel burning my soul. I dally, swimming, frolicking somehow amongst a dizzying shoal of what seem to be…. joys. I drift in the wake of a love that is huge, yet vulnerable somehow, like a whale. It is simply intoxicating. I want to remain here, to lose myself here. I can't imagine why any soul would ever want to exist in any other environment. And then I feel it.

My being shivers slightly at its initial touch. I focus on a signal that emanates from the depths below and I shudder as if maybe someone just walked over my grave. Now suddenly I sense, no, I am connected to… despair. It calls, it draws me toward itself somehow inexorably. Suddenly I no longer want to be here but I feel incapable of leaving, compelled to approach something which both summons me yet terrifies me.

The invisible rail along which I have been traveling has disappeared. My climber's rope has gone slack. I am sinking, falling deeper into what now feels like an abyss. What draws me is one and it is many. It is big and it is small. It is of this world and it is of the physical world as well. There are voices; they are spirit voices. They call, not to me in particular, but to all who may hear them. Then all at once I am at their source.

Just as with the yacht in the harbour moments before, I sense the essence of the wreck and its connections to the sea and its surrounds, I can even 'feel' its history. But even more than this, there is a connection, a line, as clear and tangible as the one I had been traveling on but which now eludes me. It is to another shipwreck, that of the ship that caused this one. In normal space and time that other wreck is hundreds of miles south of here and it lies even deeper than the three thousand metres of ocean that cover this one. Yet so strongly are these ships connected in the world I now inhabit, they feel almost indistinguishable and inseparable to me now, in this space, in this ether.

What I 'see', scattered around me like so many artifacts in the debris field surrounding this wreck, are ruined ideals and hopes forsaken. What I sense is energy, dark and powerful, rooted in frustration, anger and lust for revenge. Its touch is chilling but brings with it an intoxicating sense of focus to which I am instinctively drawn in light of my own recent loss of direction.

When the first of these ships was sent to the bottom by the second, it was considered a one-in-a-million chance shot. One shell, the first fired in anger by the killer, found the magazines of The Royal Navy's flagship and sunk her in three minutes with all hands lost, bar three. A similar 'fluke' then saw the killer herself disabled and left at the mercy of the avenging hunters. There was to be no mercy. Another two thousand men, more than perished aboard the Titanic, were to be ruthlessly slaughtered, left to drown or bleed to death.

I feel it all, the hatred, the killing, the dying. I feel the pride that once attached to both vessels, the love their crews and their nations vested in them. I feel the cheering on the days they were launched and the weeping on the days that they sank. But most of all I feel the connection between them, the lines of fate that still bind them; the lines that crossed in history, along which a single shell traveled to find a chink in the armour of HMS Hood, cutting her in half. The same lines that guided a hopeless torpedo from a quixotically pathetic bi-plane to the only spot on The Bismarck's impenetrable hull where it could do any damage: the rudder.*

These same lines now allow me to move between two sunken tombs and their histories. They threaten to bind me here in a loop of hatred for eternity. For the first time since my transcendence into this world I am genuinely afraid. I know real panic. And because I have no idea what to do, I do what people always do in such situations: I pray.

As soon as I even think of doing so it seems, the darkness around me begins to lift. I feel a lightness, a buoyancy. Suddenly, I am a floral wreath, bobbing on the waves above, set there by the comrades of the departed. It doesn't seem to matter exactly when this wreath was laid or what flag flew from the stern of the ship that laid it. Only that the rite was conducted in a solemn spirit of penitence and humility. I find it poetic that the wreath should be a hoop, just like a lifebelt.

Free of the sea and the chains of these fierce emotions, I am restored to my tramline, my climber's rope is taut once more. I am skimming the wave-tops toward the pole.

As I journey north, the floes bunch tighter together below me. Soon they form an unbroken white crust that will run all the way to the point which is the axis around which this Earth turns. It is so beautiful, the ice, neither land nor sea. I move closer to it, flirting with its essence, dipping in and out of it as perhaps a skimming seabird does on the wave tops.

I enter it gingerly, a little afraid perhaps of re-entering the water, with its over-amplified emotions, good and bad. But the ice has neither the darkness of the land nor the intensity of the ocean. Its nature is neutral, sterile in feeling and emotion. As I arrow through it, I am sensitive to the lightness of the air above it and the pull of the water below. The ice resonates, bristles, trembles like a great gossamer shroud spread over the crown of the planet. It is so thin, only a few feet thick even as I approach the pole itself. The sense of vulnerability is unsettling. I will finish the journey in the air I think.

The approach of the Pole is marked by a growing stillness of the ether in which I travel. Here at the cosmic crossroads around which our planet revolves, I have arrived at my destination. It seems fitting that it should have no fixed physical being, no rock on which man can place a flag. Here is where my climber's rope is anchored. Here is where my line of longitude ends. For here it intersects, not as geographic lines do, with other lines of longitude in the spatial horizontal. The axis of the Earth itself resonates just as the line that carried me here. I feel its passing through the core of the planet and its extension out into the cosmos and the ether, back to the beginning and beyond, out into infinity. It is along this new line I will travel from here.

And as I sink below the ice and accelerate towards the core, I know what it is to be a salmon swimming home or a sperm penetrating the egg.

Author Note

* *In May 1941, at the height of World War 2, three British warships engaged the brand new German battleship, Bismarck, in a gun battle in the Denmark Strait of the North Atlantic, north of Ireland. The first shell from the German ship found the magazines of HMS Hood, Britain's largest battleship, and sent her straight to the bottom, killing almost all her 1,547 crew. Two days later, light aircraft from a Royal Navy aircraft carrier stumbled across the Bismarck and launched a desperate, seemingly futile attack. A fluke strike by one of the torpedo planes disabled the rudder of the mighty battlecruiser, sending her back into the path of the pursuing Royal Navy fleet, just when it looked like she would make safe harbour in German occupied France.*

When the Royal Navy found her, they tore the Bismarck apart with relatively small arms fire, bombarding her for nearly three hours when a few torpedoes would have almost immediately crippled and sunk her. The bombardment and slaughter of the Bismarck's crew was retribution for 'The Hood'. The Royal Navy took virtually no prisoners, leaving those of the two thousand crew they hadn't butchered on the decks, to drown in the Atlantic on the pretext that U-boat activity had been detected in the area. It was one of the most shameful acts of the war.

John Piggott

The Coat

I hate this coat. It has a mind of its own.
At least it had until it lost it.
Now it wants to rule the world.
Well, maybe this town.
Well, at least,
it bosses me around.

I bought it out of a catalogue.
It looked great
and I was getting it half price.
Nice.
I was made up with myself.
Specially when someone
who knew
told me it was special.
"It's for sailing.
Ocean racing actually.
It's one of the best."
Now I was impressed.
But I shouldn't have been.

I mean
I hadn't got to know
about its
foibles.

Like it stands up -
on its own.
I've thrown it in the closet floor
and found it hanging up
the next morning.
All the other coats and jackets
in the corner,
shivering.

It doesn't like to be interfered with.
It's guarded
with Velcro
of industrial strength.
You'd want to be in the full of your health
to rip the pocket flaps open.
Then they rip skin off your wrist
as you fumble for car keys.
Say 'please, pretty please'
and they might
let you have them.
Then again.
They might not.
My coat seems peeved
that I haven't got
a yacht.

Everything's Velcro
for 'ease of use'.
So when you're fighting a 'breeze'
in mountainous seas
off Cape Horn,
wishing you'd never been born,
you can tighten your cuffs.
Most coats think a bit of elastic there
is enough.

cont'd >>

It insists on being neat.
And it punishes me
if I leave anything flapping.
Unsecured Velcro flaps
search
for stuff
to stick to.
Like each other.
I once caught a cuff on a lapel
and had to read a book by Houdini
to get out of it.

It's scary.
It will pick up anything hairy.
A scarf, a woolly jumper.
The cat next door.
Last week it forcibly dragged two old ladies
from the department store.

It's a boy scout.
It's prepared.
It will keep you warm
and in
and others
out.
even if all you have on is underwear.
In fact especially.
It's 'good'.
It has a hood,
that hides in the collar,
thank God.
It's neon yellow.
In case a fellow needed spotting
by the coast guard.
As if they'd rescue it.

Yesterday I figured it needed a clean.
It stood up on its own again.
With me inside it.

I took it to the washing machine
and laid into it with a baseball bat.
Even at that I had to fight
to get it inside.
When the water hit it
I think it mistook it
for the tide
or a drowning experience.

It broke out
and turned into a life raft.
It set off two flares in my kitchen.
And it unrolled its neon yellow hood.

I escaped in the helicopter.

The Deansgrange Writers

Chris Allen was born in Dublin and has been writing poetry for more than twenty years.

Tom Barrett worked in Accountancy before moving into foreign exchange with the American Express company in Dublin. In the early sixties he began selling accounting machines, leading inturn to a career in computer programming. He ran a small software house until his recent retirement. A late starter to writing, he has been with Deansgrange Writers Group for about a year.

Declan Houton is a native of Dalkey, County Dublin and a founding member of Deansgrange Writers Group. He prefers to write within the defined structure of metered rhyme, often using political/social satire for material, usually with the same human and comic touch that has made him the 'glue' of the group. He is also a committed volunteer with the Haven Partnership, a charity which builds houses in Haiti.

Fergus Kelly returned to Dublin after a number of years working in India. However, being in the export business, he continued to travel the world extensively until retirement - settling into a more leisurely and less stressful lifestyle of golf, fly fishing and walking. His experiences abroad have provided him with a most valuable and interesting background for his short story writing.

Lucille McDonald Lucille is a very special member of Deansgrange Writers Group. She joined us through a workshop the group held at The National Rehabilitation Hospital. A Health Care Practitioner in her former life, a serious car crash and brain surgery left Lucille with frontal lobe damage. Having to re-invent herself, she has done so through writing and is now a published children's author.

Padhraig Nolan is a native of County Wexford, now living with his family near Dun Laoghaire. His poems have been published in Irish, UK and US journals and he has written reviews for *Poetry Ireland*, *Eyewear* and the *Evening Herald*. He is currently making paintings, writing short stories and working towards a first collection of poetry. Padhraig maintains a (somewhat intermittent) blog at: www.pjnolan.com

Annie O'Curry is a graduate of UCD where she studied English and History of Art. As a journalist, she worked for many years writing and editing a variety of publications. She has written a guide to The Cider Industry of Ireland and has broadcast her writing on RTE Radio's *Sunday Miscellany*.

John Piggott lives on Rochestown Avenue, Dun Laoghaire and has been with Deansgrange Writers Group since its inception in 2004. A cycle shop owner in real life, he usually writes poetry, although he has also included a prose piece here. He came to writing as a form of self-therapy and practices 'flow-of-consciousness' writing by free-writing 'Morning Pages' as soon as he wakes.

Catherine Paradise is a grandmother, great-grandmother and retired nurse. Born in Scotland during the second world war, she grew up in St. Margarets, Twickenham and Wales. She is a board member of The Huntington's Disease Association of Ireland. Her interests include Bridge, reading and creative writing. Catherine is also qualified to teach cricket!

Barney Power is a native of County Waterford. While still at school, his first success at writing was winning a book token as a competition prize in the old *Sunday Press*. Writing runs in Barney's family, with four brothers also successful writers in their own right.

Caitriona Stewart Short is a native of Belfast. When she moved to Dublin she sought out other writers and became a founding member of Deansgrange Writers Group. This is her first publication.